Real Estate and Accounting for Beginners [3 in 1]

The Easy-to-Understand Guide to Invest for a Living + Accounting and Bookkeeping Tips

By

NESPY ONLINE MARKETING

for clarifying purposes only and are the owned by the owners themselves, not affiliated with this document.

Author: Nespy Online Marketing

THE GOLDEN

The Golden Inner Circle is an elitist group business incubator. It's a way to speed yourself up with far fewer setbacks. If you are already on track follow these enlighten entrepreneurs to take you to the next level of your potential.

Get the support you need to:

- free yourself from negative limiting beliefs

- develop a marketing strategy that works

- discover the Golden Method to improve your skills

- realize the dream of being able to work in complete autonomy

- create passive income with low-budget investments form your home.

The Golden Inner Circle is the movement that is leading hundreds of people to find a real strategy to achieve great results in the most profitable businesses such as Youtube, Instagram, Airbnb…

This series of over 20 books called "Clever Entrepreneurs in the XXI Century" is a step-by-step program that will take you from zero to the highest level of success.

The information contained within will help you to raise the dormant leader inside you, develop the King Midas' touch and to embody the NEW Golden YOU.

Table of Contents

Short Stays Real Estate with No (or Low) Money Down

Deducting | The Right Way

Bookkeeping and QuickBooks Made Easy

Short Stays Real Estate with No (or Low) Money Down

The 7+1 Creative Strategies to Create Passive Income from Home Using the AirBnb Business Model in 2021

By

Nespy Online Marketing

Contents

Introduction

If you are a forward-focused person, you can dream of leaving the profession to enjoy a retirement life that is simpler, or you might even consider early retirement. But a dream is only a wish without a plan. You need to contemplate passive income to put a few wheels on the dream. There are also plenty of different options for passive income and rationales of how to build it. Passive income is the money you collect that doesn't cause you to do a lot of "active" work in order to continue to earn it. In essence, you may do much of the work in advance and do some extra effort to earn an income. For instance, to keep the money flowing, if you develop an online course, you only need to update the content. Likewise, passive income strategies like renting out property and/or building a blog can take some effort to get up and running, but while you sleep, they would eventually earn you cash. You've already heard the word, "make money when you're sleeping." This is the main attraction that allows individuals to generate passive income. Even when you're not working, you can develop something (a course, a blog, e-book, videos, and/or an online store) which generates income. Or you can own something that helps you to earn passive income (property or stocks).

So why do you need to build passive income?

In the presence of a full-time job, your salary is your biggest income tool, a tool that usually requires your active involvement. Even if you enjoy your career, you wouldn't mind making some additional money without the tears, blood, sweat, and time commitment of another job. If you lose your job or want to generate an extra source of income when you are no longer productive or if you outlive your retirement fund, developing a passive income will improve your wealth-building strategy, create the opportunity to retire early, and save you from a total loss of income.

And how much money can passive income generate?

Generally, passive income won't make you wealthy overnight, so ignore those get-rich-quick schemes you've read about. But, over the long term, consistent, profitable passive income strategies will produce some serious money. Depending on the income stream, we're talking about anything from two to three thousand dollars to thousands of dollars.

Some people like to think of investing when we mention "passive income" because, with the least amount of effort, it can yield the greatest returns. But you should think about your retirement plan & passive income as two distinct subjects. The entire premise behind the long-term investment is to produce retirement income. If your fund options are good and they offer a match, you want to make sure you invest in your company retirement plan, like that of a 401(k). These are great choices for establishing a powerful pension plan, but before a certain age, you will face taxes as well as penalties for every withdrawal. You need to let your money grow only for the long term with retirement planning and not touch it. However, a form of low-effort income which can be accessed at any time should be passive income. After you are debt-free and have some cash left, one way to build passive income is by buying real estate and leasing it out to tenants. Rental property may be a fantastic source of additional income, but it is not the most passive option because, unless you employ a property management company, you will have to put a lot of effort and time into maintaining the property. You need to be in charge of your property if you go on the rental property route. Pay off your own home first before you buy a rental property, and buy your investment property with cash. You must not go into debt in order to purchase property for rent. You could develop something like an informative blog and/or a YouTube tutorial series to be able to generate online traffic if you have a bright idea that appeals to a particular audience. You might sell commercial space on your blog or ad spots on your channel if your content is engaging and it sees ample regular traffic. You can sit back, relax, and reap sources of passive income after you put in the heavy lifting. The list of ideas for passive income could go on indefinitely. Never go for any passive income strategies that promise a fast return or require large sums of money upfront. Your other financial targets would be sabotaged by them. In this book, we will present ideas that are steady, profitable, and trustworthy.

CHAPTER 1: Understand Income and Importance of Passive Income

There are three main categories of income:

Active income

Portfolio income

Passive income

1.1 Active Income

Active income alludes to money made as a result of the provision of service. Examples of active income are wages, tips, salaries, fees, and income from companies in which there is material involvement. The owner must meet the criteria for "material participation," which is based on hours worked or other factors, in order for income from a company to be considered active rather than passive. The most popular example of active income is income earned in the form of a paycheck from an employer. "Money from business activities is deemed "active" for the self-employed or someone else with an ownership interest in a corporation if it meets the criteria of material participation by the Internal Revenue Service (IRS). That implies one of the following is valid, at least:

- The taxpayer works during the year in the corporation for 500 or more hours.
- The taxpayer performs the majority of the company's work.
- Over the year, the taxpayer works for more than 100 hours in the company and no other employee works more hours than the taxpayer.

However, income earned is treated as passive income if someone earns income from a company in which they do not actively participate. Meanwhile, portfolio income is income from investments, like dividends and capital gains. Depending on the legislation at the time, these various forms of income can be taxed differently. At present, for instance, portfolio income is taxed at lower rates than active income.

Example of active income from a business

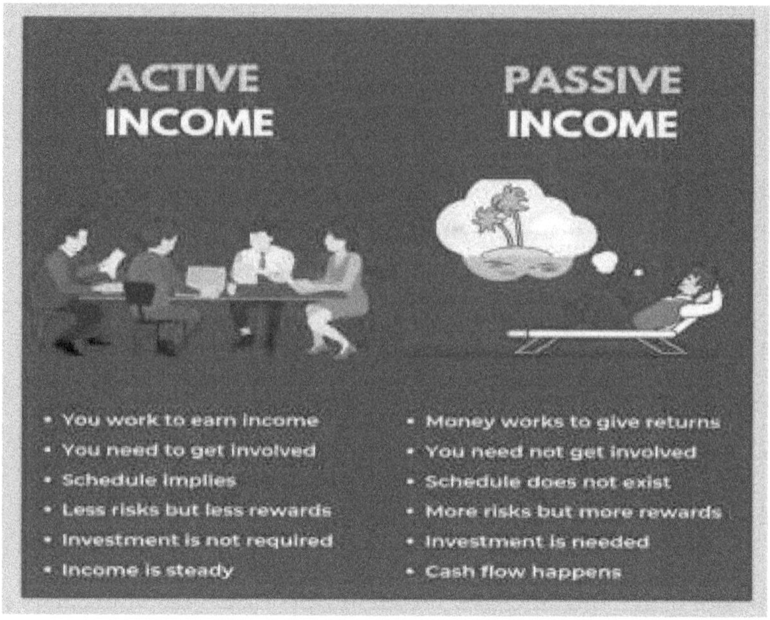

John and Laura are not married to each other. They have a 50% interest in an online business. John performs the majority of the day-to-day work in the business. Therefore, his income is considered active by the IRS. On the other, Laura helps with the marketing activities. She, however, works less than 100 hours a year in the business. It is for this very reason that her income from the business is considered passive income by the IRS. The material participation rule was established to prevent individuals that do not actively participate in a business from using it to generate tax losses which they, otherwise, could have written off against their active income.

1.2 Portfolio Income

Income from the portfolio is money received from investments, interest, dividends, and capital gains. Portfolio income streams are often known to be dividends received from investment properties. It is one of three main income groups. Active income and passive income are the others. Most income from the portfolio enjoys favorable tax treatment. Dividends and capital gains are charged at a much lower rate as compared to active income. Furthermore, portfolio income is not subject to Medicare or Social Security taxes. Income from the portfolio contains dividends, interest, and capital gains. Compared to active or passive income, portfolio income typically enjoys favorable tax treatment. Money from the portfolio is not subject to withholding from Social Security or Medicaid. One way to maximize portfolio income is to invest in an ETF that purchases dividend-paying stocks. Income from the portfolio does not come from passive investments. Moreover, portfolio income is not received from daily business activity. It is earned because of dividends, taxes, and capital gains or interest paid on loans. For tax purposes, the categories of income are important. Passive income losses can not necessarily be offset against portfolio or active income.

Ways to Increase Portfolio Income

Following ways can be employed for increasing portfolio income:

Purchase High-Paying Dividend Stocks

Investors can enhance their portfolio income by purchasing stocks that pay above-average dividends. Dividends can be paid directly to the shareholder. Moreover, dividends can also be used to buy additional shares in the company.

Purchase Dividend Exchange-Traded Funds

A cost-effective way to maximize portfolio income is to buy ETFs that explicitly track high-paying dividend stocks. For example, the FTSE High Dividend Yield Index is tracked by the Vanguard High Dividend Yield ETF. There are 396 stocks that have high dividend yields and are included in the index. For other dividend ETF options, the selection criteria concentrate on how many consecutive years the company has paid a dividend and/or on companies that have a history of raising their annual dividend payments.

Write Options

An investor can write call options against their stock holdings to enhance his portfolio income.

1.3 Passive Income

Passive income are earnings that come from a limited partnership, rental property, or another enterprise in which an entity is not actively engaged, such as a silent investor. Proponents of passive income tend to be boosters of the working lifestyle of a work-from-home and/or be-your-own-boss. Colloquially, it has been used on the part of the person receiving it to describe money being earned periodically with little or no effort. When used as a technical term, passive income is defined by the IRS as either "net rental income" or "income from an enterprise in which the taxpayer does not participate materially" and may include self-charged interest in some cases. Passive income is a source of income that may require some initial effort or investment but continues to generate payments in the future. Examples are music and book royalties and house rent payments. Passive income is the return on savings accounts. Passive income is created by a limited partnership in which a person owns a share of a company but does not engage in its functioning. Passive income consists of earnings generated from rental property, a limited partnership, or some other enterprise in which a person does not engage actively. Usually, taxes are charged on passive income. Portfolio income is perceived by a few analysts as passive income, and interest and dividends will also be considered as passive income. In order to earn and maintain, passive income needs little to no effort. When an earner puts in one of those little efforts to produce income, it is called progressive passive income. In many ways, a passive income investment can make an investor's life easier. This is true when a hands-off strategy is followed. Examples of passive income investment strategies include - Peer-to-Peer Lending, Real Estate, Dividend Stocks, and Index Funds. These four choices suggest different risk and diversification levels. As with any kind of financial investment, calculating the anticipated returns in relation to a passive income opportunity versus the loss potential is important. The main types of passive activities are explained below:

Cash flows from property income, including cash flows from a property or from any piece of real estate, capital gains, rent through resource ownership such as rental income, and in the form of interest from financial asset ownership.

Trade or business-related activities in which an individual does not engage in a company's operations other than investing during the year.

Royalties, that is, payments initiated by one corporation (the licensee) to another firm/person (the licensor) for the right to use the intellectual property of the latter (music, video, book).

Standards for Material Participation

The standards for material participation include:

- Five hundred plus more hours toward an activity or a business from which you are earning
- If the participation for that tax year has been "substantially all."
- Up to 100 hours of commitment and at least as much as every other person involved in the operation
- Material involvement in at least five of the past 10 tax years
- For personal services initiatives, material engagement at any point in three previous tax years

According to the IRS, there are two passive activity categories. Rentals, including equipment and real estate, are the first type; and businesses are the second type, where the individual does not engage materially on a daily, continuous and significant basis.

Examples of passive activities

The following are considered passive activities:

- Equipment leasing
- Limited partnerships
- Partnerships, S-Corporations, and LLCs where the individuals do not materially participate
- Rental real estate (some exceptions apply)

- Sole proprietorship or farm where the individual does not materially participate

1.4 Taxing of passive income

There are various forms of passive income, ranging from capital gains and dividends. Then the question arises whether the passive income is taxable or not. The brief response is, yes. Tax rates can differ depending on how long the assets are kept, the amount of benefit gained, and/or net income on each form of passive income.

Short-Term Passive Income Tax Rates

For assets retained for a year or less, short-term gains apply and are taxed as ordinary income. In other words, at the same rate as your income tax, short-term capital gains are taxed. The prevailing tax rates for short-term gains are as follows: 10 percent, 12 percent, 22 percent, 24 percent, 32 percent, 35, and 37 percent.

Long-Term Passive Income Tax Rates

Long-term capital gains (assets that are held for more than one year) are taxed at three rates: zero percent, fifteen percent, and twenty percent, based on your income bracket.

Taxing of real estate income

With lower tax rates, investing in real estate and high yield rental assets is now even more advantageous for individuals. The authorized business income deduction is now a twenty percent deduction on the taxable income while buying and holding real estate. This deduction of 20 percent now requires investors to subtract a portion of the real estate investment holdings, which may lead to a higher ROI.

1.5 Why Passive Income Beats Earned Income

income Earned is the income that you earn when you work the job full-time or run a business. Notice that, in most instances, "running business" doesn't require rent real estate corporate. Money gained from royalties, rents, & stakes in the limited partnerships is passive income. Income from the portfolio is the income from interest, dividends, and stock sales capital gains. Earned income would be subject to heavy taxation at all levels. Earned money should be utilized to rapidly create wealth, but your wealth must be transferred into the portfolio and passive income pools in order to reduce your tax position. Earned incomes are subject to FICA taxation and the full marginal income tax rate. There are undoubtedly ways of minimizing tax liability, such as operating an S-earned Corporation's revenue, investing in the firm and currently earning deductible expenditures, etc., but high marginal tax rates would also be subject to net income. The issue with earned money is that you still have to spend more cash in order to minimize tax liability. Passive incomes from the rental property aren't subject to the high operational tax rates. Rental property income is privileged by amortization and depreciation and contributes to a much lesser effective rate of tax.

Let's assume, for instance, you now own a rental property, which nets 10,000 dollars before the depreciation & amortization. Let's just say that $8,000 is the total amount of depreciation and amortization. It leaves with a taxable revenue of $2,000. You can pay a tax equivalent to 740 dollars if you fall in the 37 percent tax bracket. Yet you see an effective rate tax of just 7.4 percent as we equate the $740 with the amount raised ($10,000). If you made the same 10,000 dollars in the earned income, in order to minimize the amount available to tax, you would need to expend more. Otherwise, with $10,000 into taxable income, you'd pay $3,700, meaning you're in 37 percent tax brackets. With the rental real-estate, every year, you don't have to be paying for depreciation. It's a ghostly cost which you have to claim. That's why, from a tax standpoint, passive income knocks out earned income.

1.6 Reasons Why Passive Income Is So Important

It's no wonder passive income's, and for a good cause, one of the most thought about, sought after aspects of personal finance. Passive income will have an incredibly positive effect on only about any financial situation, from creating vast wealth to avoiding a paycheck-to-paycheck lifestyle. But that poses the question: why does passive income matter so much? In short, passive income's essential because in financial life, it provides flexibility, prosperity, and independence. In addition, because your time & resources do not limit passive income, it may have a beneficial and important impact on the ability to build wealth. Passive income, in different words, is 1 of the easiest ways to upgrade the financial condition. But if that's not compelling enough, we've listed the top reasons why passive income's important.

Improved financial stability

One of the most significant milestones you will hit on the road to prosperity is monitory stability. In different words, even if you really can see your financial position and realize, with certainty, that you're capable of coping with a powerful financial storm, so then you're on a very stable path. If you may count on the money rolling inside without having to fight for every cent of it, even more than that, so financial security is just a nearby corner. More money which comes in more you can be secure and comfortable in the finances. It helps you in relaxing, look at the bigger picture, & make smarter financial decisions because you don't have to grind for every dollar you earn, which, in turn, increases your financial health. This is a magnificent little cycle & one of key reasons why passive income is playing such a major role in personal finance.

Less reliance on a paycheck

The discomfort that comes with living paycheck to paycheck is not comparable by any means. And if it is your case, then one of the best moves you can take is to add a bit of the passive income in your life. There is no secret in that sometimes it may get a bit stressful as you trade time for dollars. And the more you will distance yourself from a focus on the next paycheck, the lighter it can be in your life. One of the greatest advantages of passive income is avoiding the paycheck-to-paycheck lifestyle.

It's easier to achieve your goals

Did you ever say to yourself, " only If I made extra money, then I could accomplish my monetary goals much more quickly..."? Well, that's just another explanation why the passive income's so awesome. It doesn't what financial targets you're trying to attain; you can accomplish your goals much quicker if you build certain passive income sources that enable you to make money all the time of day.

More freedom to pursue your passions

You will unexpectedly find yourself with the opportunity to pursue your passions or, for that matter, your ideal job, along the same line as avoiding the paycheck to the paycheck lifestyle, while you get some of the passive income flowing through the bank account. Remember that it's easy to end up trapped in a position you can't bear when you focus on the active income to make ends meet. It is tough enough to leave a career. But it is particularly tough to leave a job if you don't have sufficient money to pay the rent that is due in two weeks. On the other hand, you have the opportunity to do the things you really want to do when you have a stable stream of passive income running into the finances of yours. Passive income, to put plainly, offers you choices. & with those choices, independence comes.

Location independence

Likewise, in many ways, passive income encourages you to live and working from anywhere you like. Since you don't have to work constantly to earn a passive income, so you don't have to be working from a particular position either. You could tour the world if you like, as far as you earn passive income sufficient to support your lifestyle. And plenty of people do.

Early retirement

Retirement is, to some degree, for many people, that may only be done later in life. Although, if you're building any passive income sources, retirement may not be far away as you thought. Really, if you love the thought of retirement at a young age, so then your primary financial priority should be passive income. If it means creating a company that operates even without you needing to be present there, participating in real estate, or a mix of few different sources of income, if you desire to stop working at a young age, passive income is necessary.

More financial margin

more financial margins you will build in life, better off you will be in personal finance. In different words, the more distance you've between the expenditures & your income, the better it will get for financial life. And when you produce a constant stream of the passive income per month, it becomes much simpler to build the financial margin. Let's say, for instance, that your monthly gross expenditures increase up to 3,000 dollars. Now, if you're earning $4,000 inactive household revenue, then the monthly margin is $1,000. Yeah, that's not bad. However, if you add an additional $2,000 in passive monthly income in to the mix, life just got a lot better.

Reduced stress

There's one unity between all, after everything we've spoken about so far. It's plain; passive revenue has a distinctive way to reduce the financial burden. A passive income life is considerably less difficult than a life deprived of it. Because your financial security, margin, independence, and too much more are improved by passive income, it's only logical that it will help alleviate your financial burden. So, if financial condition makes you feel a little tightened around the collar, you may just want to give passive income a little more priority.

It's exciting

Passive income is not constrained by the effort and time that you can put into it. In different words, at all the hours of night and day, passive income can be earned, including while you are sleeping. Yet, at the same time, making money is incredibly thrilling. There's nothing like waking up in the morning thinking that you've won a few hundred bucks while you're sleeping. And the more you are enthusiastic about the financial condition, the more probable you are to continue to improve it.

CHAPTER 2: Passive income ideas to help you make money in 2021

Passive income may be a wonderful way of helping you produce more cash flow, & global upheaval created primarily by the pandemic is evidence of the importance of having many income sources. Passive income lets you cross the gap whether you unexpectedly become jobless or even whether you willingly take the time from work away with the pandemic tossing the working condition of most people into disarray. You might get the cash rolling in from passive income even while you follow your primary career, or if maybe you can build up a good passive income pool, you may need a little to kickback. Anyway, you are granted additional protection from passive income. And if you are concerned about being capable of saving enough money to reach your retirement objectives, accumulating capital through passive income also is a tactic that could be appealing to you. Regular earnings from a party other than the employer or the contractor are counted as passive income. IRS (Internal Revenues Service) notes that passive revenue will come from 2 sources: a company or a rental property in which one is not directly participating, such as paying book royalty or dividends on securities. Most individuals agree that passive income's about getting more for nothing. It's got get-wealthy-quick charm, but it also includes work in the end. What you offer is work upfront. You may do any or all the job upfront in practice, but the passive income also requires some extra labor along the way too. To keep the passive dollars flowing, you might have to save your merchandise updated or well-maintained rental property. But if you're dedicated to the approach, it could be a perfect way to make income, and by the way, you'll build some more financial stability for yourself.

2.1 How many streams of income should you have?

"When it comes to generating revenue sources, there is no "one size fits all" advice. How many revenue streams you have can depend on where you are financially and what your potential financial targets are? But it is a decent beginning to get at least a handful. "With multiple lines in the sea, you'll attract more fish. Rental assets, revenue-producing shares, and company ventures are a perfect way to diversify your income stream, in addition to the earned income produced by your human capital. You'll want to make sure, of course, that bringing work into a new passive income stream would not cause you to lose sight of the other sources. So, you want your efforts to be aligned and make sure you pick the right options for your time.

2.2 Passive income ideas for building wealth

So, if you're considering building a passive income source, look at these techniques and absorb what this takes to succeed with them, whereas still recognizing the dangers involved with each strategy.

2.3 Selling information products

One common passive income approach is to produce information products, such as e-books, or video or audio lessons, and then kick back while cash rolls inside from product sale. Via platforms such as Skillshare, Udemy, and Coursera, courses could be distributed & sold. Otherwise, you may think of a "freemium model"-making a free content follow-up and only charging for the more comprehensive details or for the ones who wish to learn more. Language teachers or

/ & stock-picking guidance, for instance, can use the model. Free material serves as a demonstration of talents and can draw those who want to be going to the next stage. You may use advertising (or sponsor) to make your revenue as the third alternative for this concept while offering information or material on a free forum like YouTube to a growing audience. Take the love of music or video games, for instance, and transform it into the content.

Opportunity

The Information products will have an outstanding revenue stream, so after the initial time outlay, you quickly make money.

Risk

development of this product typically requires a huge amount of effort. And it needs to be good in order to make great money off it. There isn't space out there for trash. If you wish to be competitive, you must create a strong base, advertise your products & prepare for other products. Unless you get very lucky, one product isn't business. Generating more outstanding products is the easiest way to market an established good. You could create a strong income stream once you understand the business model.

2.4 Rental income

A successful way of earning passive income is to invest in rental properties. But more work is always needed than people expect. You could risk your money if you do not take the time to know how to create a profitable venture.

Opportunity

If you want to earn the passive incomes from the rental properties, then you must determine three things:

- Financial risk of owning property.
- Property's total expenses and costs.
- How much profit you need on investment.

For example, suppose your objective is to make $10,000 in a year in the rental income. At the same time, your property has monthly mortgages of 2,000 dollars and charges another 300 dollars in one month for the taxes & other expenses. In this scenario, you will have to cost 3,133 dollars in the monthly rent for accomplishing your objective.

Risk

few questions should be considered: Is there a marketplace for a property? How if you have a homeowner who pays off the property late or harms it? Suppose you cannot rent the property out? The passive income could be significantly impacted by any of the variables. And pandemic also has raised new threats. You could suddenly have occupants who could no longer afford their rent because of the economic crisis, although you may already have a mortgage of your own to be paying. Or, if earnings fall, you couldn't be capable of renting out homes for as far as you did before. So, to secure yourself, you'll want to consider these threats and have a contingency plan in place.

2.5 Affiliate marketing

However, with affiliate advertising, website owners, "influencers" on social media or blogs support the goods of third parties by including a link to the product on the forum or the social media network. The best-known associate partner maybe Amazon, but Awin, ShareASale and eBay, are all among the bigger brands. And for those watching to develop a following and sell goods, TikTok and Instagram have become major websites. To attract attention to the blog or else steer people to goods and services which they may like, you might also start growing an email list.

Opportunity

The site owner receives a fee if visitors click on the link and make a transaction from a third-party associate. The commission may vary from 3-7 %, so it would obviously need substantial traffic to the site to produce serious revenue. But you could be able to make some serious coin if you may expand the following or even have a more profitable niche (like tech, fitness, or financial services). Affiliate advertising is deemed passive, and, in principle, only by adding a link to your social media platform or website, you will gain money. In fact, if you cannot draw readers to the site to tap on the link and purchase anything, you won't earn anything.

Risk

You'll have to be taking time to develop content and generate traffic if you're just starting out. Building a following will take important time, and you'll need to discover the best formula to reach the crowd, a task that could take a while on its own. Worse, the audience might be likely to fly to the next famous influencer, topic, or social media site after you've expended all that energy.

2.6 Flip retail products

Make use of online sales sites like Amazon or eBay, and offer goods you find nowhere at prices of cut-rate. You will arbitrage the difference between the prices between your purchase & selling, and you will be able to create a following of the people who monitor your transactions.

Opportunity

The price disparities between what you'll find & what average customer will be capable of finding would encourage you to take advantage of them. If you've contact that may help you obtain affordable goods that some other individuals can locate, this might work extremely well. Or you might be capable of uncovering useful products which others have completely missed.

Risk

Although deals can happen online at any moment, you'll probably have to rush to find a reputable source of goods to help keep this strategy passive. And you're just going to have to know the competition so that you don't buy at a price that's too much. Otherwise, in order to market, you can finish up with goods that nobody needs. Moreover, you may be forced to slash the price drastically in order to make the product worthwhile for the buyers.

2.7 Peer-to-peer lending

Peer-to- peer (or P2P) loan's personal loan supports by the intermediary of third-party like LendingClub or Prosper between you & borrower. Funding Circle that targets firms & has greater borrowing caps, and Payout, which targets better collateral losses, are other players.

Opportunity

You generate income as a lender from interest payments made on loans. Yet, you face the possibility of default because the loan is insecure, implying you might end up with nothing. You must do two things to cut the risk:

By paying smaller sums on different loans, diversify the lending portfolio. Minimum investment for each credit is $25 at Prosper.com and LendingClub.

To make educated choices, evaluate old data on the prospective borrowers.

Risk

It takes time to learn the lending metrics of P2P because it's not completely passive, and you'll want to vet your prospective borrowers closely because you ought to pay particular attention to payments earned when you're engaging in several loans. If you intend to create profits, whatever you make for interest can be reinvested. Economic recessions may also make the high-yielding personal loans more likely to default candidates because if the COVID-19 manages to harm the economy at higher than historical rates, these loans will go bad.

2.8 Dividend stocks

The Shareholders in companies with dividend-yielding securities receive a payout from the company at regular intervals. The Companies pay the cash dividend out of the earnings on a quarterly basis, and what you need to be doing is to own stock. Per-share of stock, dividends are funded, meaning the more shares that you hold, the larger your compensation.

Opportunity

Since stock income is not linked to any operation other than the actual financial investment, it may be one of the most passive ways of money-making to own dividend-yielding securities. In your bank account, the money will simply be deposited.

Risk

Choosing the correct stocks is a tricky aspect. Without carefully researching company issuing stock, too many novices leap into the market. You have to study the website of each organization and be acquainted with their financial statements. 2 to 3 weeks you can spend researching each venture. That said, without wasting a massive amount of time analyzing firms, there are some ways to participate in the stocks dividend-yielding. ETFs, or Exchange-traded fund, are strongly recommended for income generation. ETFs are hedge vehicles containing collateral such as equity, commodities & bonds but trading like stocks. The ETFs are an excellent alternative for novices because, due to much lower prices than mutual funds, they are easier to understand, affordable, highly liquid, and offer much higher potential returns. Another key risk's that the stocks or the ETFs will decrease dramatically over short periods of time, particularly in times of volatility, such as when the financial markets were shocked by the Coronavirus crisis in 2020. Economic uncertainty may also cause certain firms to fully cut the dividends, while the diversified funds can experience less of a pinch.

2.9 Create an app

Creating an app may be a method to invest time in advance and then enjoy rewards over time. Your software may be a game or one that allows smartphone users to execute any feature that is difficult to do. Users download it once the application is public, & you can generate revenue.

Opportunity

There's a big upside to an app if you can create something that captures your audience's fancy. You'll think about how it's best to generate revenue. You could run in-application advertisements, for example, or else make users pay a small fee to use the app. You'll definitely add incremental improvements to keep the product current and popular as the app gains attention or you get feedback.

Risk

Perhaps the greatest risk here's that you spend your time unprofitably. You have no financial drawback here if you contribute little to no money to the project (and/or money which you'd have spent otherwise, for instance, on hardware). It's a competitive market, though, and genuinely popular applications must give consumers a persuasive benefit of experience. If your app gathers some data, you would also want to ensure that it is in accordance with privacy rules, which vary across the globe.

2.10 REITs

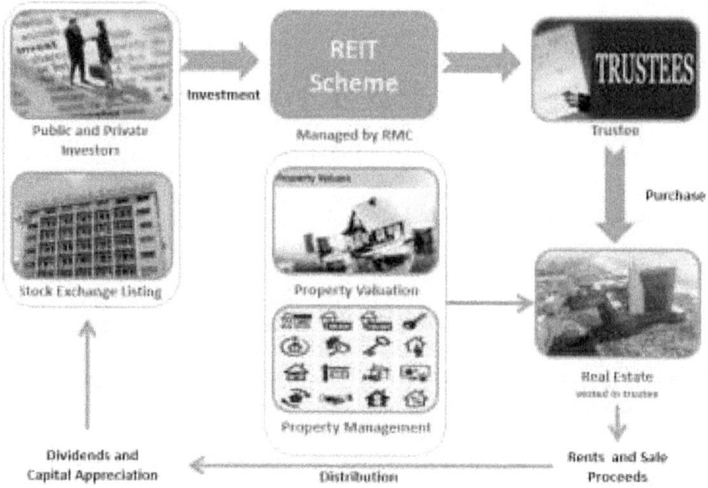

For a corporation that owns and manages real assets, REIT is a real estate investment trust, which is a fancy word. REITs have a special legal arrangement such that although they pass over any of their income to owners, they pay no or little corporate income tax.

Opportunity

In the stock exchange, you can purchase REITs much as every other business or dividend stock. You're going to earn whatever the REITs payout as a payout, and the strongest REITs have an annual record of growing their dividend, meaning over time, you might have an increasing supply of dividends. Specific REITs could be more expensive, like dividend stocks, than buying an ETF composed of hundreds of REIT stocks. Fund offers instant diversification, which is inherently much better than owning specific stocks & you can always earn a good return.

Risk

You'll have to be capable of selecting good REITs, much like dividend stocks, that means you'll have to evaluate any of the firms you might purchase, which indeed is a time-taking process. Also, while it is a passive activity, if you do not know what you're doing, you might lose a lot of money. And neither are REIT dividends safe from difficult economic times. If REIT does not produce enough income, this would possibly have to slash or totally remove its dividend. So just when you want it, most of the passive income could get hit.

2.11 A bond ladder

bond ladder's sequence of bonds maturing over a number of years at various periods. The phased maturities help you to reduce the risk of reinvestment, which is a risk of locking up your cash as bonds offer interest rates that are too low.

Opportunity

bond ladder's a traditional passive investment that for decades has attracted near-retirees and retirees. You will sit back to collect the interest payments, and you "extend the ladder," transferring the principle into different package of bonds as the bond matures. For starters, you could start off with one year, three years, five years, and seven years of bonds. In the year that 1st bond matures, you have two years, four years, and six years of bonds left. You may use proceeds from the newly aged bond to purchase another one year or roll out an eight-year bond with a longer-term, for example.

Risk

Bond ladder reduces one of the big dangers of purchasing bonds, the possibility that you may have to purchase a new bond as the bond develops when the interest rates will not be attractive. Bonds, too, come with the other risks. Although the federal government backs Treasury bonds, corporate bonds aren't, meaning you could risk your principal. And to diversify the exposure & eliminate the risk of someone bond harming your total portfolio, you'll want to buy multiple bonds. Many investors move to bond the ETFs because of these issues, which include a diversified fund of bonds that you may put up on a ladder, removing the possibility that a single bond will harm your returns.

2.12 Invest in a high-yield CD or savings account

Investing in an online bank's high-yield deposit certificate (CD) or savings account will help you to produce passive income and get one of the country best interest rates as well. In order to make money, you won't even have to leave home.

Opportunity

You'll want to do a fast check of the nation's great CD rates or the top savings accounts to make the most of your CD. Going to the online bank instead of the local bank is typically far more advantageous since you will be able to pick the highest rate available in the region. And if the financial firm is backed by the FDIC, you will also receive a fixed return of principal of up to 250,000 dollars.

Risk

Your principal is secure as far as the bank is backed by FDIC and under limits. So, it is just as secure a return as you'll find to invest in a CD or savings account. Nevertheless, though the accounts are secure, these days, they return even less than before. And with Federal

Reserve aiming at 2% inflation, the least in the short run, you're going to miss out on inflation. A savings account or CD can, though, yield less than keeping your cash in cash or in a non-interest paying checking account where you will earn about zero.

2.13 Buy Property

Real estate can be a decent way to make a passive income, depending on where you invest and when. There has been a rapid growth in the value of property in common cities such as Toronto-44 percent in Canada alone in the last five years. You will find some lower-cost properties by purchasing pre-construction condos, which will rise in value by the time it is eventually completed, enabling you to sell the property once it is complete for a profit. Like for all investments, it can be dangerous, so if you're new to the market, it's better to talk to a real estate agent to help you purchase the correct investment property.

2.14 Rent out your home short-term through Airbnb

This simple approach takes advantage of space that you don't need anyway, and converts it into an opportunity to make some money.

Whether you're leaving for summer and/or have to be outside of the town for some time, or maybe even you want to fly, try renting your present space out while you're gone.

Opportunity

On a variety of websites, including Airbnb, you may list space and set rental conditions yourself. With limited additional work, you'll receive a check for efforts, particularly if you rent to a tenant who might be in place for a couple of months.

Risk

You do not have a lot of financial downsides here, but it's a gamble that's atypical of the most passive investors to let strangers stay in your house. Tenants can, for instance, even deface or ruin your property or steal valuables even.

2.15 Air BnB Business as a Passive income Strategy

Airbnb is an online website for selling and renting urban homes. It ties hosts and travellers and promotes the rental process without owning any rooms on its own. Moreover, it cultivates a cooperative economy by allowing private flats to be leased by property owners. Airbnb is an internet platform which links individuals that wish to rent the homes to an individual in that area who are searching for a room. It currently surrounds more than 100 thousand cities in the world and 220 countries. The name of the business derives from the "air mattress B and B." Engaging in Airbnb is a way for hosts to gain some money from their home, but with the possibility that it may be damaged by the visitor. The benefit could be comparatively cheap lodging for visitors, but with the possibility that property wouldn't be as advisable as the listing has made it look. For less than the cost of a hotel bed, travellers may also book an Airbnb. The traveler's biggest concern is that the property could not live up to its listing. The primary concern for hosts is that their property may be badly damaged by guests.

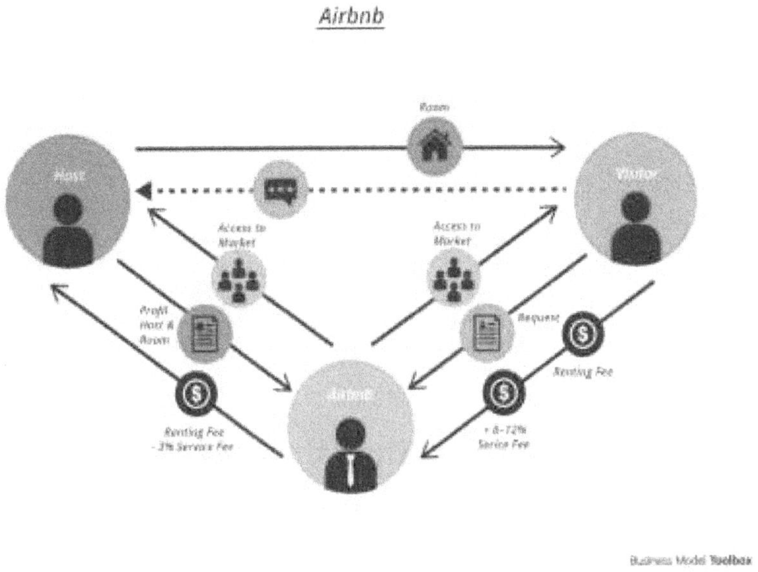

The Advantages of Airbnb

It offers the following advantages:

Wide Selection

Airbnb hosts list several different categories of properties on the Airbnb website, like single rooms, a suite of rooms, moored yachts, , whole homes, studios, houseboats, even castles.

Free Listings

In order to list the assets, hosts don't have to be paying. Listings may contain written descriptions, captioned photographs, and user profiles so prospective visitors can have the knowledge about hosts a little better.

Hosts Can Set Their Own Price

It is the host's prerogative to decide how much to charge per night, per week, or /and per month.

Customizable Searches

The Guests can filter the Airbnb database and not only through date & location, however also by price, property type, amenities, and the host's language. To further limit their search, they may also add keywords (such asclose to the Louvre').

Additional Services

Airbnb has increased its services to include events and restaurants in recent years. In addition to a list of available hotels for the dates they expect to visit, individuals searching by the venue can see a list of opportunities provided by nearby Airbnb hosts, like classes and sightseeing. Restaurant listings also contain Airbnb hosts' reviews.

Protections for Guests and Hosts

As a protection for customers, before transferring the funds to the host, Airbnb keeps the guest's payment for 24 hours following check-in. For guests, Airbnb's Host Guarantee program "provides security for up to $1,000,000 in damage to covered property in eligible countries in the rare incident of guest damage."

The disadvantages of Airbnb

It has the following demerits:

What You See May Not Be What You Get

Booking Airbnb accommodation is not like booking a space with a big hotel chain, where you have a fair promise that the property will be as described. Individual hosts, though some may be more truthful than others, create their own listings. Previous visitors, however, often post updates about their experiences, which may offer a more critical perspective. To make sure the listing is correct, review the reports of other guests who have stayed at the Airbnb house.

Potential Damage

The greater concern for hosts is potential that their property will be damaged. Although most stays go without incident, when the Airbnb hosts assumed they were renting to a peaceful household, there are reports of entire houses being trashed by thousands of partygoers. Some insurance is offered by Airbnb's Host Guarantee program, mentioned above, but it does not cover anything, like cash, rare artwork, jewellery, and pets. Also, hosts whose homes are destroyed can experience significant inconvenience.

Added Fees

A number of extra charges are imposed by Airbnb (just like, of course, hotels and other lodging providers). To cover Airbnb's customer care and other programs, travelers pay a guest management fee of 0 percent to 20 percent on top of the reservation fee. Prices are shown in the currency that the customer chooses, provided it is sponsored by Airbnb. Banks or issuers of credit cards can, where applicable, add fees. And though listings are free, to cover the cost of handling the transaction, Airbnb charges a service fee of at least 3 percent for each reservation.

It Isn't Legal Everywhere

Would-be hosts need to review their municipal zoning codes before listing their properties on Airbnb to make sure it is legal to rent their properties. To receive special permits or licenses, hosts may also be required.

2.16 Advertise on your car

By merely driving your car across town, you can be able to raise some additional income. Contact a specialized advertisement firm to determine your commuting patterns, like when and how many miles you drive. The firm will "wrap" your car with the ads at no cost to you if you're a match with one of their advertisers. Newer vehicles are being searched by agencies, and drivers should have a clear driving record.

Opportunity

If you're still putting in the miles anyway, though you may have to get out and drive, then this is a perfect way to earn hundreds every month at little to no added expense. It is reasonable to pay drivers by the mile.

Risk

Be extra cautious about locating a reputable operation to work with if this idea seems good. In this space, many fraudsters set up schemes to try to bilk you out of thousands.

2.17 Invest in Stocks

When you look at the wealthiest people in the world, it's pretty fair to conclude that their deep, endless savings accounts are a result of their major investment in stocks. Warren Buffett reads 500 pages a day, but he doesn't read your usual mystery novel. He reviews the annual corporate reports. He better knows whether or not a company is doing well by reviewing annual reports each day, which helps him improve his decision to invest in stocks. While the act of investing in stocks is very passive, the analysis that goes into it is active. Nevertheless, investing in shares will help you gain passive income that goes well beyond what your value is worth at your 9 to 5 work. So, if you enjoy reading about the success of different firms, consider this passive income approach.

2.18 Make Your Car Work for You

Driving is another everyday practice that you can translate into passive income. When you're just walking around, why not pick up a commuter or two to run errands? Uber can help you make money by taking people to their designated destination by driving your vehicle. You may also put ads on your vehicle to collect cash as you drive around. When your car is not used while you're on holiday, driving, or just during a normal workday, it will still make money. You will make thousands of dollars with an app like Getaround by renting out your car if you're not using it. Plus, drivers of Getaround vehicles get the best parking spaces in town, a $50 monthly rental credit on any vehicle they want, and one million U.S. dollars in primary insurance coverage.

2.19 Sell your Videos

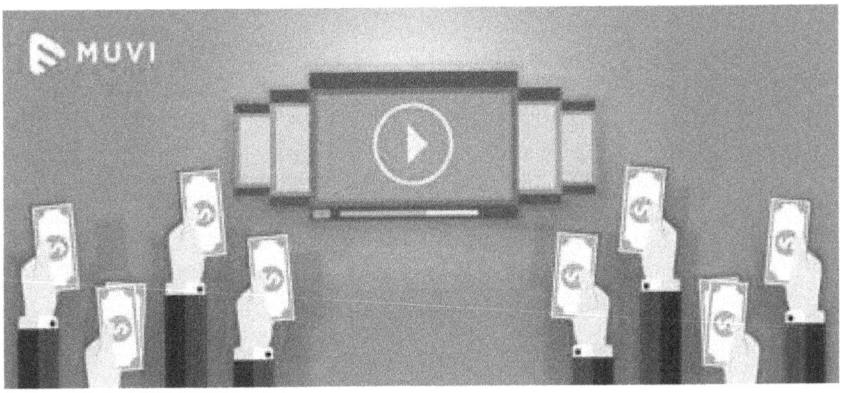

We live in a day and age where video content fascinates hundreds and thousands of humans. You would want to take out your phone and hit the record if you still find yourself in the middle of drama and excitement. To allow you to make some passive income, you can sell stored content. Why? It is because the video can be sold to a news site. And you can make some recurring income for weeks, months, and maybe even years if the video takes off. Of course, being at cultural gatherings such as marches, rallies, and festivals is the best way to get in on the action. You'll find ways for your material to be sold anywhere there's controversy. And corporations will pay you to make viral videos along with providing a share of total earnings if you are successful at creating engaging content.

2.20 Create YouTube Videos

The passive income source that just keeps on giving is YouTube. You'll find that you can make a regular income from your YouTube channel, from funded videos to ad sales. Creating videos on a regular basis for a long time is the key to creating a profitable YouTube channel. If you stick with it in the long run, you will finally start reaping the benefits of passive income.

2.21 Write an eBook

In 2009 and 2010, e-books came onto the scene and are now a hugely successful content medium. While they first became popular a few years ago, to this day, there is still a very decent chunk of individuals who make passive income from writing e-books. It's an insanely dynamic business, of course. Yet, you might find yourself with a nice slice of the profits if your writing chops are stellar. You could build a fanbase of loyal readers by designing how-to e-books on famous niches and marketing them.

2.22 Sell Digital Products

You can make digital goods if you're trying to create your own products rather than selling someone else's. You can sell your digital goods online using Shopify. From e-books, educational classes, PDFs, custom graphic templates, stock images, or some other digital goods, digital products will contain anything. Selling these items is the epitome of passive income, and with immediate updates, the whole operation can be streamlined on Shopify.

Car Wash

Car wash is a perfect way to earn a semi-passive income. Although a car wash will need daily cleaning, it is something you can either contract out or do once a week. We are talking about the very simple car wash that is cinderblocks, a pressure washer, and the powered coin, as a side note. It's certainly a corporation vs. a passive income stream if you're trying to run a drive-through car wash.

2.23 CPC Ads (Cost Per Click)

You get really paid whenever anyone clicks on your link and signs up for something or orders something through affiliate ads. On the other hand, show advertisements charges depend on the volume of traffic and eyeballs that you receive on their ads. On the other hand, for CPC advertisements, also known as "cost per click" ads, anytime someone clicks on an ad, you get paid no matter what they do after that. You don't have to hope or pray that they're buying anything or signed up for something. Any single click takes money into your account with the bank. Does that mean that all day long you can go to your own website and click on ads? It is not realistic since the corporation will inevitably find out what you are doing and cut you off. With all that in mind, it should not be a part of your plan here to click on your own ads. Instead, aim to build up traffic so that more and more viewers every day see the ads.

2.24 Minimize your taxes on passive income

A passive income may be a wonderful side-income generation strategy, but you can still create a tax burden for your effort. But by setting yourself up as a business and building a savings portfolio, you can reduce the tax bite and plan for your future, too. However, this solution will not work with all these passive strategies because to qualify. You will have to be a legal organization.

Register with the IRS to make your company receive a tax identification number.

Then call a broker, such as Charles Schwab or Fidelity, who will open a self-employed retirement account.

Determine the type of savings account that will fit well for your needs.

CHAPTER 3: Airbnb Offers The Best Passive Income Generation Strategy

rental vacation industry is rising quickly. It is real quick indeed as a matter of fact. The sector is currently generating 57,669 million dollars in sales, according to recent analysis reports from Statista.com. The revenue is awaited to grow to a market value of 74,005 million dollars by 2023 and is projected to see an average growth rate of 6.4 percent. This data illustrates just how broad & robust the holiday rental management industry is. And you should expect demand for Airbnb property management to pursue to grow over the coming years with the growth of Airbnb rental properties in recent years. Therefore, if one day you are aiming to become a manager of Airbnb property, now is a great time to be entering the business. But how are you able to get started? We will supply you with what you have to know regarding how to be an Airbnb vacation rental property manager. We're going to teach you what this takes to handle rental Airbnb properties, particular instruments you're going to be needing before you start, and stop points for the beginners for achieving successful property management. So, without further ado, over here are all six steps to beginning an Airbnb property management career in real estate.

3.1 Understand the Vacation Rental Industry

Just like some other business, without learning at least the fundamentals of this area, you can't succeed. However, no formal qualification is necessary to become an Airbnb property manager, and many find success with the only diploma of high school in this profession. Thorough knowledge of how the holiday rental industry & Airbnb run is what you need to have. So, if you don't already have it, having this information now is the 1st step to being the manager of the Airbnb properties. Ideally, as Airbnb hosts yourself, you should have some experience. If you've already hosted your rental property on Airbnb, run it yourself, you can show to potential buyers which you know exactly what you are doing. Furthermore, this will allow you to be prepared better to predict challenges, recognize potentially troublesome travelers, and cope with common issues. But if you don't have the experience, through online guides and classes, you can empower yourself about the rental vacation industry & how Airbnb works. There are plenty of those out there that can help you create a good base on which you have to learn. For instance, you may take marketing coursework to know how to extend your scope and get bookings more and business courses to know how to manage a company, keep records, & file tax. As an Airbnb property manager, it'll help you improve your creditability. Before you start, another significant point to learn is where the Airbnb hosts invest in rentals for the short-term. You'll know the place to find customers looking for management support with this detail.

3.2 Create a Maintenance Management System

Managing rental of short-term rentals ensures that you'll get visitors checking in & out repeatedly. One of many duties of the property managers, of course, is to review property before visitors visit & after they depart. Every now & then, operators of holiday rentals must also conduct repairs to ensure that the properties are in perfect shape. This is vital to ensure the happiness of both your customer and guests. For instance, imagine having visitors who had parties and had rental property trashed before leaving. Nobody with such a situation is going to be happy to step into a rental. As a consequence, before addressing the issue, the manager of Airbnb property can never leave the maintenance as an afterthought or even wait for the property owner to receive several inquiries. In addition, to offer high-quality care on their behalf, great short-term property rental operators often work alongside a dependable maintenance team. Your staff should include, among others, plumbers, house cleaners, and electricians. For any check-in, these entities will ensure that Airbnb assets you handle are tip to top.

3.3 Put Together a Vacation Rental Marketing Strategy

The most significant tasks of property managers are promoting and selling holiday rentals to attract prospective visitors. Today, there are millions of listings on Airbnb & more rental sites for the short-term, which is creating rivalry among the Airbnb hosts. It is why one of the first things potential users would like to know is how you're going to get reservations and increase their occupancy rates for Airbnb. As a consequence, you must have a basic comprehension of tactics and methods for property marketing. Therefore, having a marketing campaign that will draw Airbnb visitors to the holiday rentals you run is the next step towards being Airbnb properties manager. Start by writing an enticing listing that will maximize the probability of retaining a high rate of occupancy & a positive flow of cash. To make rental properties under your management stand out, think about investing in advanced photography & videography facilities, also branding services. Moreover, selling holiday rentals suggests that you have to go outside the listing platform. It is why active rental managers of Airbnb use social media and also SEO to meet the target tenant audience. If you don't know how it works, before you begin handling rentals in the short term, we strongly suggest that you begin to read about real estate marketing.

3.4 Invest in Property Management Tools

You can handle them with hard work and a few spreadsheets as you become manager of Airbnb property for the first time when you have only some rental properties underneath your belt. This becomes difficult, though, as you continue to add more assets to manage. How are thirty check-ins & cleanings going to be done in 1 day? At an early point, it is best to begin thinking about it so that you're planning yourself & your company for success and expansion. Using real estate management of property software that allows to automate & remain structured is the best approach for this.

In order to operate their businesses more effectively, modern holiday rental property supervisors rely a lot on technology. There are several high-tech solutions that make it easy to handle Airbnb rental, from the smart lock to invoicing, pricing, and the guest screening software systems. You will even find holiday rental apps which will synchronize schedules and handle multiple Airbnb profiles for free from different platforms. Not only does the use of such instruments make your life more effective as a manager of real estate properties, but they can also give you the strategic edge to keep rising. Mashboard, for instance, is a software that lets managers of Airbnb property connect with their customers and find the right properties for those to expand their business.

3.5 Outline Your Guest Management Strategy

Amazing client care is one of the abilities that any manager of real estate property wants to provide when handling both conventional and holiday rentals. It is how effective operators of Airbnb assets set themselves away from the audience. A good selling point, particularly for Airbnb travelers, is customer service that goes beyond and beyond. Getting a guest engagement plan ensures that during their visit, the services can be open to visitors and their demands at whatever time. Expect the short-term visitors to have to inquire or inquire over something. You must be capable of responding in a timely way to such unannounced requests. How can you treat a case, for instance, where the visitor has misplaced keys to a holiday rental and can't get in? There will be a contingency in it and other cases for a successful Airbnb property manager. In addition, to manage communication with visitors, managers of top-performing properties also have automation tech systems in place. Airbnb guests really enjoy great customer service & show this by posting favorable feedback. This, in essence, helps to get more bookings & boost cash flow, that will surely make the customers happier. As you could see, one of the most critical skills for good management of Airbnb property is definitely customer service, so don't consider it as an afterthought.

3.6 Set a Reasonable (But Competitive) Price

To become a manager of Airbnb property, the only thing you need is a pricing plan. Usually, the holiday rental manager takes a percentage cut from the real host's secured rental fee. A selection of online outlets recommends anywhere from ten to twenty-five percent. At the same time, others believe that more consumers would be drawn by charging the lowest price; that isn't the case. Customers base their options on the quality o facilities rendered by property managers-not dependent on costs. Thus, providing the lowest price means that you don't have top-tier facilities for owners of Airbnb property. You need to take several factors into account in order to fix the correct price. First of all, as stated, is what kind of services you are providing. Naturally, for something that you don't sell, you do not charge. Look at experience instead, what distinctive points of selling you may give, and set rate accordingly. The local economy and what the other rental property (short-term) managers in the area charge, the seasonal demands, also current events, you will need to remember. Ultimately, you need to set a fair price which you are sure will be getting you back that your service is worth.

3.7 How an Airbnb Business Works

Nearly everyone has listened to Airbnb or has used it. It is the platform for online home rentals that helps hosts renting vacant private short-term accommodation from a single room to whole homes. Airbnb launched in 2007 & has expanded exponentially to have listings in further than 65 thousand cities in the world with more than three million available properties. Here is how to start a sustainable Airbnb company if you have sufficient rental space and are searching for additional revenue. Through uploading photographs and details of the room for rent, the first move is to be a host on Airbnb and register the home. When an Airbnb property's listed, travelers searching for a room in the host area will access it. Guests may use a number of requirements to check for Airbnb listings, like:

- Availability dates
- Destination
- No. Of rooms, such as bedrooms and washrooms
- Price
- Host language
- Amenities such as hot tub, breakfast, pets allowed, and etc.
- Facilities like air conditioning, parking,etc.

Prior to booking the chosen space through the Airbnb guest may establish a contact with hosts directly for gathering additional information through the Airbnb service of messaging.

Access

Along with browser access, Airbnb offers mobile applications for Android and Apple IOS devices.

Security

For security purposes, the hosts are expected to provide Airbnb with appropriate identification. Travelers should post the reviews of hotels to create a trustworthy group (and the hosts may review the guests). The Reviews aren't anonymous.

Guest Services

Airbnb offers a stable payment platform for the guest's calmness of mind, and fees to the hosts are deferred until 24 hr after the arrival of the guest. In the event that any difficulties are faced during the renting time, Airbnb has a 24-hour hotline for the guest.

Fees

Host sets the price for lodging. Moreover, Airbnb charges under-mentioned fees:

Host: Three % transaction payment fee

Guest: six to twelve % booking fee

The Hosts can also ask for a security deposit & could well charge a cleaning fee.

Taxes

Airbnb could apply provincial, state, or city taxes for guest bookings depending on the jurisdiction.

Travelers Prefer Airbnb Rentals

One of the best things about operating an Airbnb company is that, for several reasons, travelers choose Airbnb over motels, hotels, or hostels:

Cost: Usually, Airbnb rent is much inexpensive than a similar hotel room. In certain instances, an entire house may be rented through Airbnb for the cost of a single suite of the hotel, depending on the location.

Living locally: Living the life of a local person is the key advantage of the Airbnb service. Most guests of Airbnb choose to stay inside the community and explore the destination way the locals do, instead of renting a generic hotel room.

Privacy: customers of Airbnb are not continuously surrounded by visitors and workers at the hotel.

Peace & quiet: the Airbnb rents are usually more secure and do not suffer from loud hotel events, such as guest exits early in the morning, young children, maid service, and traffic.

Witness what you get already: Unlike a hotel where you can see a snapshot of similar rooms on their Airbnb page at best, you get full images and explanations of the real premises.

Diversity: From yachts and boathouses to castles and lighthouses, Airbnb has an immense variety of available accommodations.

Home comforts: Airbnb has a homey atmosphere of a real living space instead of generic hotel spaces (few have resident pets even). Kitchens allow the guests to cook their own food if they desire to save money on outside dining or have dietary issues.

Friends or Family: Through Airbnb, you may save a lot of money by renting a whole apartment/ house/condo rather than the multiple rooms of a hotel for family and friends.

Is Renting Your Space Permissible or Advisable?

Ensure you're legally permitted to be an Airbnb host into jurisdiction before you plan to start an Airbnb business, & you're prepared to respect local laws & regulations. Depending on the state/ city or regional rules, municipal laws governing the hosting of paid visitors will vary greatly; they are absolutely banned in some areas whilst they're subject to occupancy tax in others if space is condominium or apartment, check to view if it is allowed to sub-let the premises. There are also regulations in place for apartment landlords & condominium societies to prohibit an owner from renting the units out as Airbnb rooms. Renting your apartment out without the knowledge of your landlord will have you evicted. Neighborhood ties are also a significant concern. In the area, a few inconsiderate or loud Airbnb guests will easily turn you in a pariah. If none of the challenges are insurmountable, it could be an outstanding opportunity of home-found business to become an Airbnb host.

Are You Committed to Becoming a Host

There are a variety of additional concerns to remember prior to making a definitive decision to host Airbnb:

Would you like to start a business? Then Starting an Airbnb company is like establishing any business- that you need enthusiasm, entrepreneurial spirit, & the ability to make the required effort, starting off with doing relevant background analysis and developing business plans.

Do you've energy? It could take a great amount of time to be a landlord, particularly for the short-term rents. You'll have to:

- Manage reservations and reply to interactions with prospective tenants.
- Plan to meet the guests to give out or receive keys
- ensure the property, including fresh linen, breakfast supplies, is cleaned properly and ready for the arrival of the guest (if applicable)
- Fix some property maintenance problems such as plumbing and pest control, electrical & appliance repair
- Be accessible to the visitors on a 24 into 7 basis if the property has any problems.

Demand: The deciding factor in the popularity & price of rented accommodation is visitor demand. The highest places for rental returns are:

sought-after tourist destinations with high hotel rates (famous neighborhood ranks higher on the Airbnb searches)

situated Centrally, close to visitor attractions, shops & public transport,

Featuring panoramic views and facilities like parking, balconies, etc.

Seasonality: Demand for the property in the northern hemisphere will definitely drop drastically in winters (unless you're renting a ski chalet). In comparison, rental accommodation demand in colder southern locations (like Arizona) decreases dramatically in summers.

What are the marketing aims? Are you trying to earn a little cash or create a stable income on the side? The financial portion of the business plan must show target market analysis and reasonable forecasts of your property's future rental income. The income from the Airbnb contract depends upon:

Before you start thinking about leaving your job & making a living through running an Airbnb company, make sure that by seeing rental prices & booking regularity for comparing Airbnb listings of your area, you carefully examine the revenue potential of your property.

Extra costs: In addition to booking fees paid by Airbnb, there are extra costs involved with Airbnb hosting, including:

Insurance: Standard insurance plans for homeowners do not include the use of the property for commercial uses, including renting on Airbnb. Airbnb has a free host compensation insurance policy in Canada, U.K., U.S., and many other nations, offering up to 1 million dollars in guarantees against personal harm or property loss. If your place is not protected by Airbnb policies, please contact your insurance provider to see if there is sufficient coverage.

Business Licenses: Airbnb hosts are being required by more & more cities to hold a business license.

Repair and Cleaning: You want to keep rental properties in top condition all the time in order to keep your Airbnb host ranking at a high standard, which includes extensive cleaning during guest stays and daily repairs. The charges will contribute to your expenses if you have to sub-contract cleaning and repair duties.

Listing and Pricing Your Property on Airbnb

Accurately describe the place and make this stand out. Note that Airbnb is an online marketplace & you have to be thinking like a realtor to make listing stick out from the competition in order to optimize guest interest in your house. Start by looking at the same Airbnb listings inside the region and consider the amenities/features and prices listed. If this works, make a spreadsheet. The definition of your listing must be precise, comprehensive, complete, and highlight, which makes it special. Comprehensively define the facilities and functionality of your room also as any regulations or preferences of visitors. Providing high-quality photographs of the room is incredibly necessary. Airbnb has specialist availability of photography service in certain places if you are unable to do this yourself.. You don't want visitors to be upset because the room isn't as advertised or you've exaggerated amenities. Note that the guest rankings would be partially dependent on the accuracy of your listing description.

Price Your Listing Competitively

You should also get an idea of how to market your listing from your analysis of similar listings. It needs to be competitively priced to keep the property consistently booked (and increase profits).

Improving Your Host Ranking

Higher the property pops up in rankings, the more probable it's to be chosen by visitors, so having good rankings of Airbnb is crucial to the success of Airbnb business. Airbnb rankings are like internet search rankings. And by building confidence and offering a fantastic experience to your visitors, you will boost your rankings.

Build Trust

Airbnb community's based on trust and guests would be searching for hosts with contact information, credentials, and favorable feedback.

Verification

For the new hosts, verification is highly essential: change your profile and include other details like the email address, phone number, Facebook profile, and etc. For giving prospective visitors some confidence that you're a reliable host.

References

You should post the references from colleagues, co-workers, relatives, business partners, etc., to build more trust. For the other Airbnb users, you may even write references.

Provide Great Customer Service

Like any entrepreneur would tell you, the cornerstone of any successful business is customer care, and becoming an Airbnb host has no difference. Positive ratings, better search scores, and more bookings reward hosts of Airbnb who have the best experience of the guest. The hosts with the most popular are:

Responsive

The Hosts that can not be bothered for responding in a timely manner (or at some) to inquiries are a big turnoff for visitors. In reality, Airbnb keeps track and rates your replies to guests accordingly. With higher search rankings and improved bookings, the host who has the highest ratings of response is awarded. At all times, Airbnb mobile application will help you to keep connected. All the time when visitors are present, be available through phone and check up with them on extended trips and see if there's something more you may do to maximize the services.

Update Their Calendars Regularly

Keeping your calendar current, also enhancing the guest experience, boosts the Airbnb rankings of search.

Fix All Problems quickly

When a guest mentions problems like leaky taps or a burned-out lightbulb, it should be repaired promptly and render an apology to the guest. Sure ways to boost the guest rankings is to provide five-star service.

Act on Their Reviews

Fix the issue and benefit from the failures if a visitor writes a critical review. React to complaints all the time in a respectful way.

3.8 The Bottom Line

In real estate, there are many ways of earning profits. The growing success in the U.S. housing sector of Airbnb and other short-term rentals has created opportunities not just for real estate developers but also for property managers. Today, there is a great demand for vacation rental managers, and industry analysts expect that over the coming years, there will be national growth. Therefore, imagine being an Airbnb property manager if you're looking for a profitable means of generating passive income.

Conclusion

In a nutshell, passive income is money that comes at regular intervals without having to invest a large amount of work into generating it. By blogging, one method of producing passive income may be achieved. If you've figured out how to produce content that attracts sufficient traffic to the host advertising, you can make a product that your customers would want to purchase. From a basic e-book to a sophisticated app that produces sales for several years after it is released, passive income could be anything. Similarly, people have a lot of things, and they still look for cheap places to store this. What might be simpler than asking people to pay you for storing their things? An investment on a large-scale in purchasing storage facilities (with the cash) or anything simple like offering the basement or the shed might entail creating passive income by offering storage. All you'll need is to make sure their goods are clean and stable. You will make money by selling them to others against such charges if you've any things that you don't use at all times, which others will love to borrow. As rental items, useful items such as a tractor, trailer, kayak, trampoline, or your own lawn even may give you passive income. With the support of platforms like Airbnb, this also involves renting spare rooms out in your home. Upload the pictures of items, fix a date, and tell the world they're ready for the rent on your favorite social networking site. The reason why it is necessary to have passive income is that it will help increase your financial consistency. The more passive income you make, the easier it becomes to be consistent with your financial life, from consistently saving to consistently spending to consistently donating. One of the strongest and most relevant aspects of a sound financial condition is passive income. It is beneficial for you in several ways, from enhancing your financial health to reducing your financial burden.

Deducting | The Right Way

Untangling Small Business Accounting and Taxes Based on Online Activities

By

LEONARDO BLANCO

Table of Contents

Introduction

You'll definitely have to do a lot of day-to-day daily duties, including accounting, when you first launch your small online business. Knowing how to track and forecast your business's income and expenses is a valuable skill for growth, so familiarise yourself with the basics of accounting.

And if you're willing to outsource your accounting and bookkeeping right now, learning the fundamentals can help you appreciate your finance professional's findings and correctly evaluate your company's financial wellbeing.

We've broken down all you need to understand about small online business accounting, including how to monitor and evaluate your business's main financial indicators, in the parts below.

Chapter: 1 Online Business and its importance?

There has never been a better or easier time in history to start your own business than now. Everyone is connected now, regardless of their income status or geographic location, thanks to the development and growth of easy-to-use website creation tools and social media.

Whether you are rich and powerful or impoverished, you can now freely share your abilities and connect with people around the world. It can also be very inexpensive and simple to get started for those looking to start an online business.

Many people have started online businesses for less than 200 dollars. (the cost purchasing a domain name, hosting service and professional theme).

You can start a business if you can connect with others and fill a need.

In fact, there are numerous advantages to starting and owning your own online business, ranging from increased income and freedom to assisting others in achieving their own personal goals; however, in order to keep things simple and to the point, I will only go over seven of the many advantages to starting and owning your own online business.

1.1 The importance of eCommerce

1. eCommerce Helps You Reduce Your Costs

To make your online store, it isn't essential that you have every one of your items introduced in an actual space. There're various organizations that work online where they just demonstrate all their stock through their electronic business.

This suggests not just saving by not requiring a purchase or rental of premises, yet besides all that includes electric power, the internet, and so forth or then again in the event that you need to have one, so clients have an actual space, it doesn't need to be just about as extensive as all that you offer. Regardless, you'll reduce your expenses.

2. eCommerce Helps Businesses Go Global

Straightforwardly identified with the previous point, this reality permits you to put your items available to be purchased anywhere on the planet. They won't have the express need to venture out to where you're to perceive what you've to bring to the table.

If you're running an actual store, it'll be restricted by the geological zone that you can support, yet possessing an eCommerce site will offer you the chance to expand your effort. It will offer your items and administrations to clients around the entire world, paying little heed to the time zone and distance.

Besides, this wipes out a wide range of topographical and etymological tango hindrances. Your online business converted into various dialects will permit them to purchase from various nations.

With eCommerce & mobile business also, the whole world is your jungle gym. Your services and products are accessible for many clients sitting on another edge of the world.

In this way, if you need to develop your online business worldwide, it is a good thought to begin making your online store & localize it in various dialects.

3. eCommerce Can Also Be Done through Fewer Overheads and Fewer Risk

Beginning an online store might mean essentially bring down expenses of a start-up contrasted with a physical retailer. The retailer or the online entrepreneur does not need to think about the shop rent high costs, employing a sales associate to facilitate the client, efforts, service charges, safety, and so forth. This, can empower you to sell them at good costs. Moreover, an online shop allows you to grasp expanded productivity with less danger.

4. eCommerce Can Broaden Your Brand & Expand the Business

Having some eCommerce store can be used to widen the scope of items or administrations available to be purchased, extending your business, bringing you a huge number of customers, and broadening your deals. It is the ideal method to take a personal brand from a conventional block & mortar store to a novice, all-around adored one.

With eCommerce, there's no compelling reason to have more than one branch, only one particular online store permitting you to completely arrive at clients without agonizing over moving areas; you can deal with your online business from home.

It's imperative to specify that eCommerce will be useful for Both B2B & B2C businesses to help personal brand mindfulness in the online market.

5. eCommerce Offers Better Marketing Opportunities

Your eCommerce website is the best advertising device that you could at any point have. On a web account, anybody can advertise via online apparatuses such as web-based media advertising, email promoting, web search tool advertising, pay per click advertisements, and SEO assists you in constructing valuable connections & contacts.

For instance, with great SEO, your online store will show up in the top searches of SERPs. Likewise, online media organizations will give you a stage to draw in and construct trust with your clients through audits and appraisals, just as keeping them acknowledged with normal posts about your items and offers.

6. Your Online Store Will Stay Open 24*7/365:

Additionally, one of the incredible significances of eCommerce that eCommerce merchants can appreciate is store timings are currently all day, every day/365 as the eCommerce stores are working 24 hours per day, 7 days per week, contrasted with the customary stores.

Along these lines, merchants can expand their deals by boosting the number of requests. Nonetheless, it's additionally useful for clients when they can buy items and administrations at whatever point they need, whether it's early morning/midnight.

7. eCommerce Is Easier & More Convenient

Individuals' lives are rushed; getting to an actual store implies taking a ton of time and exertion. In this way, beginning an online store implies you can find a way into your client's bustling lives, making the items they need available when they need them.

The agreeable thing about eCommerce is purchasing those choices that are fast, simple, helpful, and simple in understanding with the capability to move supports on the web.

"In web-based shopping, your product is consistently a single tick away instead of actual shopping where you might be compelled to hang tight for quite a long time or months before a product you requested is accessible," says Heritage House, who sell kid suits on the web.

On account of eCommerce's accommodation, shoppers can save heaps of time, endeavors just as cash via looking for their items effectively and making buying on the web.

8. Personalize Your Shopping Experience

In the event that there is one of the unmistakable favorable circumstances of having an online store, you will have the option to know what your buyer does. Genuinely, it would be entirely awkward for a likely purchaser to enter your store, and you were constantly behind him, inquiring what he needs or for what valid reason he doesn't accept your item.

Web-based business permits you, for instance, to know when in the process you left the buy midway and even recall that you left it in the center by sending an email. This, also, can assist you with improving your shopping experience for other events: shortening the means to finish the request or offering those purchaser items with comparable attributes.

9. Improve the Image of Your Business

Among the benefits of having some online store, there's no uncertainty that it likewise incorporates improving the picture of your organization. Offering a decent online deals stage to clients will give your organization an extraordinary corporate appearance.

Not exclusively will it end up being state-of-the-art; however, it will likewise show interest in encouraging buyer buys. For instance, it keeps you from making a trip to the actual spot of offer and permits you to analyze costs from home. Likewise, because of what we have referenced as devotion or input, you can even actualize upgrades in your items that clients will esteem emphatically

10. Easily Receive Feedback on Products

Have you generally needed to understand consumers' opinions about what you are selling to offer more or make it greater? Indeed, the online store will permit you to get that input to actualize enhancements in the business, through star appraisals, with the chance of leaving remarks.

Also, the client will feel heard after their buy. There could be no greater method to thank you for your trust in buying your organization's items. Besides, in the event that you offer the quality, you'll have nothing to stress over. Empowering an immediate channel where others notice what they can anticipate from the given resource is an extraordinary public illustration of trust in online business.

11. Maximum Security of Transactions

Today, working on the internet is practically more secure and dependable than doing this in an actual store. From home, without anybody watching on your mysterious number or Mastercard. The eCommerce site should have an SSL endorsement.

This testament not just permits safe perusing on the website. What's more, it keeps the information scrambled to be protected to add keys & passwords. This won't just be important for the client's business account yet to utilize much more touchy information, for example, Mastercard data with complete, true serenity.

It merits referencing that 33% of eCommerce specialists distinguished security, versatile installments, and portable applications as the main interests in 2019. Security will keep on being one of the best spotlights on eCommerce.

With changes in innovation, client practices, and shopping designs, dealers should give arrangements guaranteeing the trust and security of shopping measures.

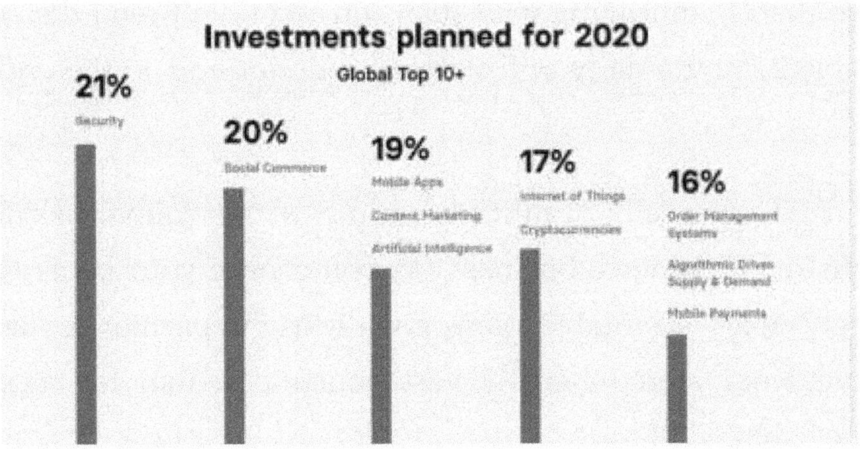

12 Ready for the Trade of the Future

It's another significant detail considering the long haul of the business. Search customer spending and patterns, the headway of innovation, and the most recent insights gauge that by 2040, 95 percent of buys will be executed through the web.

Along these lines, it's not just discussing a pattern of the present yet additionally about what the business relations of things to come will be. Furthermore, similarly, as though you are not on the internet, you don't exist; if your business doesn't sell on the web, it is monstrously restricting its deals.

13. Increase in Sales

Everything mentioned previously is centered around a certain thing: having the option to build your deals. At the end of the day, the business relies on selling more, and in this way, what it will be based on.

All the past focuses add to the way that the 10th and last bit of leeway are that there's an expansion in the acquisition of your items. Arriving at more clients, improving your items on account of remarks, or being accessible 24 hours daily will without a doubt add to the entirety of this.

As a rule, it's normally beautifully simple, with minimal risk and cost to begin an eCommerce business. As you choose your benefits/items incisively, have a suitable plan, got the right partner to help you construct your store, there is very much potential for automated revenue & high ROI.

Chapter: 2 Accounting and Its Purpose

Accounting is the structured method of defining, tracking, assessing, classifying, checking, and transmitting financial records. It shows a company's profit or loss over a specified time, as well as the value and quality of its assets and liabilities, as well as its shareholders' equity.

2.1 Why is Accounting Important?

Accounting is very important and necessary for small business owners because it requires owners, administrators, investors, and other stakeholders to determine the company's financial results. Accounting provides key facts regarding profit & loss, costs & earnings, assets & liabilities for decision-making, scheduling, and risk management within an organization.

Accounting's main goal is to document financial transactions in books of records in order to recognize, calculate, and transmit economic results. Furthermore, tax reporting authorities mandate you to maintain simple books that track profits and expenditures.

2.2 What Is the Purpose of Accounting?

Accounting is regarded as the "Language of Business." It is a system of communicating financial information to multiple uses for decision-making purposes. The major objects of accounting are:

1. **Recording transactions**

Accounting's primary purpose is to control a systematic, accurate, and full record of a company's financial activities. The accounting system's backbone is made up of these reports. When appropriate, company owners should be able to review and evaluate transactions.

2. **Budgeting and planning**

Business owners must prepare how they can distribute their limited resources, such as workers, cash, machinery and equipment to meet the company's goals.

Budgeting and planning, an integral aspect of business management, enable companies to prepare accordingly by forecasting requirements and resources. This assists in the coordination of multiple corporate segments.

3. **Decision making**

Accounting assists in a variety of decision-making processes and facilitates business owners in developing policies to improve business process efficiency. The price to be charged for products and services, the resources required to produce these products and services, as well as financing and business opportunities are all examples of decisions based on accounting information.

4. **Business performance**

Business owners may use financial records to assess how good their organization is doing. Financial reports provide a credible tool to evaluate important performance indicators, encouraging business owners to compare their output to that of their rivals as well as their past performance.

5. **Financial position**

The financial statements issued at the end of the accounting period represent a company's financial position at the time. It displays the amount of capital invested, the number of funds utilized by the company, the profit and loss, as well as the number of assets and liabilities.

6. Liquidity

Mismanagement of funds is a common cause of small business failure. Accounting assists in assessing a company's liquidity, which is characterized as the cash and other liquid capital available to pay off debts. Via the identification of bottlenecks, the information lowers the risk of bankruptcy.

7. Financing

Accounting assists business owners in the preparation of historical financial records and also financial forecasts that may be utilized while preparing for a loan or securing investment.

8. Control

Accounting assists in avoiding losses attributable to stealing, fraud, mistakes, injury, obsolescence, and mismanagement by enforcing different checks within the company. Internal monitoring secures the company's finances to eliminate long-term risks.

9. Legal requirements

Businesses must retain correct financial statements of their activities and disclose those records with shareholders, tax officials, and regulators, according to the statute. The financial statements and details are often needed for the filing of indirect and direct taxes.

Chapter: 3 Why Is Accounting Useful for Small Business Owners?

One of the most common causes of small business failure, especially in the first year, is poor financial management. Accounting plays a critical role in providing information that assists small companies in their growth and advancement when they have a restricted budget and other resources.

Accounting is important for small business owners for the following reasons:

- Maintain a careful watch on the cash balance. You should enforce strategies for effective record-keeping and a solid financial strategy to prevent the company cash flow from running dry.
- Cost management may help small business owners grasp the principles of fixed expenses, variable costs, and how to correctly cost a project. This way, you won't waste funds on a project you felt would be profitable.
- Accounting helps you to have a clearer view of the company's health. Learn to interpret a balance sheet, financial statement, and cash flow statement to do this.
- It helps you in identifying and avoiding consumer, employee, and supplier bribery and stealing.
- You'll be more able to tackle investigations if you grasp corporate accounts and transactions.

- When working with corporate leaders who have a strong grip on the company's finances and are mindful of the financial consequences, bankers are more comfortable.

If you're a sole proprietor or have workers, the trick to expanding your small company is to monitor your financial records on a routine basis and build a comprehensive budget that helps you to recognize operating inefficiencies. Saving a little money on a few things will add up to a lot of money in the long run.

Chapter: 4 Accounting basics How to Run a Successful Online Business

A painful task is accounting. It is the dull side of the business. But you can't ignore it if you want your business to grow. You could try to dump all your receipts into a drawer and hand them over to a stranger. Yet you are going to give them financial power. That means losing your business's future. You will hand them a sweet slice of change to do it all for you, too. I guarantee it isn't as hard as you may be afraid of, though. And, for day-to-day operations, you shouldn't require an accountant. You should still know the fundamentals yourself, even though you are paying for guidance. You may acknowledge and challenge what someone is talking to you in this context. It's your business at stake, after all.

The following accounting fundamentals help you need to know to grasp your money.

1. **Get Accounting Software**

Don't bother using excel or a calculator to piece it all together. Do yourself a favor and get software for accounting. FreshBooks are sold to clients that operate e-commerce businesses. Or there are a variety of accounting software apps you should get right in their app store if you use Shopify. Your business and interests would rely on the right choice. Make sure you choose a bookkeeping system while you're shopping in the app store. Look for software to monitor revenue, expenditures, and inventory. Keep away from programs that generate invoices only or include reports only. You want a tool that's able to do everything for you. Select one that can sync directly to your ecommerce store, whether you want apps like Shopify or go for something different. It would make things even better.

2. **Monitor Cash Flow**

Get one if you don't have a separate bank account with your business yet. You need to realize that making money is your job. And watching the cash balance is the best way to see this. When you've got more coming in than heading out, you actually do well, don't you? The timing of money going out and coming back can also be monitored. After all, what if, tomorrow, all your bills are due? When you have one million rolling's in next month, it won't mean a whole lot if you can't pay the workers by then. Bear in mind any investments on your accounts that you have. What ways of payment do you give your clients? Are some of them putting a grip on the money? From the moment a consumer spends to the time the money is in your accounts, is there a five-day delay? When you're finding out when you have resources to spare, you ought to remember this. For monitoring currency, Shopify offers a free template. With Excel, you can quickly build your own.

Per week, monitor what you plan to spend. Track the money that you plan per week to come in. You realize you're going to have a challenge if what you need to pay is more than the new bank balance and what's coming in. To improve to boost your cash flow, adopt these tips:

- Do not spend anything sooner than you have got to. If it is due within thirty days, compensate it within thirty days.

- To ensure revenue stays through, suggest selling recurring payment contracts or subscriptions to consumers.
- Hold a reserve 'just in case' in your company bank account.
- Do not overcomplicate yourself. You do not require massive statements of cash balance.

3. **Determine how inventory should be counted**

Ignore this step if you're selling a service. Inventory is the product that you sell or all the materials that you use to make that item. Do not forget to include any costs for your product being wrapped or packaged. Decide what minimum inventory volume you want to have on hand, and make sure you are tracking inventory before you pass this point so you can reorder. The last thing you want is for inventory to run out and lose sales.

Why does inventory form part of the basics of accounting?

Money equals inventory.

It is the money you spent buying that stuff. You will not make any money back until you sell your product. And while it is sitting in your warehouse, the money tied to your inventory can change (or store, or apartment).

If I purchase 50 items for 100 dollars each, and the price rises up to 150 dollars tomorrow, then immediately, my inventory is worth more.

So, if tomorrow's price falls to 50 dollars, the worth of my inventory is less.

And beware of 'shrinkage'!

That's why, unexpectedly, you have fewer inventory than you should have.

You know you've purchased 50 items. You understand that you sold and delivered 40. You should be left 10 items, right? What if you have only 8 left? This is shrinkage. Perhaps an item was misplaced, or robbed, or destroyed and had to be discarded away. There are plenty of explanations for why this happens. When you don't have a physical department location, the positive thing is the shrinkage is smaller. Currently, factory shrinkage is pretty poor. Less than 1% of the overall product is a normal shrinkage. It's also less probable that you will have shrinkage if you're running a business out of your house. After all, if you're the only person around it, you are less likely to see anyone rob the inventory. Compared with a large warehouse, it's also a lot tougher to lose stock in an apartment. Having said that, shrinkage will happen to everyone. This is why it's necessary to routinely physically count inventory. If you have missed 100 dollars worth of goods and factor it into your accounting, you ought to know.

CGS, which means cost of goods sold, is an expense directly linked to the goods sold by you. This is inventory sold, and also how much it costs to produce that inventory. Suppose say there is one widget you sell. The cost of goods sold for that widget should be whatever it costs you for the parts and also whatever it costs to build it. If the widget parts cost 60 dollars, the packaging cost is 15 dollars, and you paid someone 15 to put it together, that the total cost of the widget will 90 dollars.

MATERIAL COST	60$
PACKAGING COST	15$
LABOUR COST	15$
TOTAL COST OF GOODS SOLD	**90 $**

4. **Calculate all Expenses**

You already understand that the costs are directly tied to the volume of sales. Next, you need to know how much it costs you for anything else. Any costs that do not grow as you sell more or drop when you sell fewer are known as 'fixed costs.' Let's say If you pay a monthly rent, for instance, the price is set. If you sell one widget or a million, it won't shift. Such costs are not part of the cost of the goods sold, and the profit margin is not compensated for. However, they do control your earnings and your cash flow.

Some Common fixed expenses are

- Utilities
- Rent

- Interest on loan payments
- Property Tax
- Wages

These expenses are considered a fixed expense because even though you sell nothing next month, you have to reimburse them. Do not confuse this with an expense where every month is the very same amount. An expense such as electricity may be more than one month longer than the next. Or maybe there's more to it in winter than in summer. In accounting standards, it is always a fixed expense. You will use an average for budgeting if expenses change month to month.

5. Find out Break-Even Sales

Budgeting and planning are essential aspects of operating a business. Next, you are not only going to want to know if last month you made a profit, you are going to want to know if this month and next you want to earn more.

Your break-even sales amount is the amount of sales dollars you need to earn to cover all your costs.

Let's assume, for instance, all the fixed costs add up to 5,000 dollars a month. This ensures that you have to sell enough of the product to meet the cost of producing it (including labor cost) and also an additional 5,000 dollars only to break-even (no profit, no loss).

Break-Even Sale = $\dfrac{\text{Fixed Cost}}{\text{Revenue per unit} - \text{Variable cost per unit}}$

$$= \frac{\text{Fixed Cost}}{\text{Unit Margin}}$$

If your break-even number of units are 5,000 and you sell only 3000, then you are in problem. And if break-even 5000 and you sell 7000, then you are in a good position.

6. Schedule your right tax rates for customers

Here is the aspect for which most citizens groan: taxation. Taxes are necessary, and they may become very complex. At this point, you may want to contact a tax consultant specialist, if you sell a number of various goods & services to a lot of people around the world. Thankfully, systems these days are fairly smart. For you, the software can take control of much of this.

7. Prepare your Tax Payments

Now, if you are properly set up to collect tax, you also need to make sure you are ready to pay it. Your tax laws will rely on where you are located, actually. At a minimum, believe that as much tax as you have earned must be submitted. This suggests that it is necessary to consider that money of tax is set aside. If not, then when you submit tax return, you face some hurdles. Many online shopping platforms allow you to pay tax on your purchase price, such as Shopify.

For example, if you buy a product that price is 100 dollars and the tax rate is 20%, then you will pay the amount included tax.

Product Cost	100 $

Tax Rate (15%)	15 $
Total amount included Tax	**115 $**

8. Balance Sheet

At the end, you must understand your balance sheet. We have already addressed all as well as cash balance on the income statement. The balance sheet is the final thing to cover. This is what helps you watch the long-term performance of your business and see how your business is performing in general. An income statement is a timely overview. The broader image is a balance sheet. Assets, liabilities, and equity make up the balance sheet.

BUSINESS CONSULTING COMPANY
BALANCE SHEET
As at December 31, 2015

Assets		$	Liabilities & Stockholders' equity		$
Current assets:			Liabilities:		
Cash		85,550	Notes payable		5,000
Accounts receivable		4,700	Accounts payable		1,600
Prepaid building rent		1,500	Salaries payable		2,000
Unexpired insurance		3,600	Income tax payable		3,000
Supplies		250	Unearned service revenue		4,400
Total current assets		95,600	Total liabilities		16,000
Non-current assets:			Stockholders' equity:		
Equipment	9,000		Capital stock	50,000	
Acc. dep. - Equipment	3,600	5,400	Retained earnings	35,000	85,000
Total assets		101,000	Total liabilities & stockholders' equity		101,000

I have finally discussed all the accounting basics you should be practicing day to day and month to month. Start with simple accounting software. It can make your life a lot easier.

Then, note that cash is king, and keep a grip on your cash flow. You should be doing this on a frequent basis unless you have a large cash reserve built.

Next, you ought to consider the revenue, expenditures, and earnings. This is your income statement, which lets you know whether you are earning money per week, month or year.

Do not neglect to schedule for taxation. Set up the e-commerce platform to receive them if you need to. Place the money together to reimburse them should you need to.

Finally, construct the balance sheet. Or let the accounting software do it for you. This will help you exactly how 'healthy' the business is long term. It's a simple way to know if you have so much debt.

There are plenty of other accounting rules and methods that will help you save money at tax time.

There will also be reporting options that can be addressed whether you're seeking to get investors or a loan for growth.

But for running your company, don't get pulled into the complicated laws. It will only distract you from your crucial day job of operating your business.

An accountant will assist you with something beyond and above the fundamentals if you require to.

Chapter: 5 Common Accounting Mistakes and How to Avoid Them

Numerous new business visionaries handle their bookkeeping and accounting when they are beginning. Here are how to stay away from some normal DIY bookkeeping ruins.

When numerous business visionaries first begin, they attempt to deal with their bookkeeping to set aside cash. Notwithstanding, following each penny of pay, costs, charges, and seller installments are messy and tedious. Errors can happen effectively & they can charge your huge business loads of cash.

To help you forestall these monetary blunders, the absolute most regular bookkeeping ruins are below that entrepreneurs make and – all the more significantly – how to keep away from them.

1. Lack of organization

Accounting requires extraordinary association abilities. You'll need to record each exchange, digitize or store receipts for future reference, figure duties, and the sky is the limit from there. In case you're not appropriately following or putting away data, you'll probably miss a significant exchange or lose a receipt, which could get you into difficulty come season of tax.

2. Not following a regular accounting schedule

With the wide range of various duties, you have as an entrepreneur, refreshing your books may tumble to the lower part of your plan for the day. Notwithstanding, it's imperative to set a normal timetable for including late payments and costs. While every day refreshes are ideal, you ought to, in any event, enter your exchanges consistently.

3. Failing to reconcile accounts

While you are recording monetary information and income in your books, you need to routinely return and guarantee your ledger mirrors that equivalent equilibrium. In the event that there's a difference between the two, there's likely a mistake that requires quick thoughtfulness regarding keep the issue from deteriorating. Consistently exploring your business financial balances against your books can likewise help you get any fake exchanges that may have happened.

4. Ignoring small transactions

It's not difficult to disregard that little thank you blessing you sent to a customer or the ream of printer paper you got on your way back to the workplace. Regardless of how immaterial the exchange is, it's critical to record it & get some receipt. In case of an assessment review, you should have the option to give the IRS records of all your costs of doing business, even the little ones.

5. Not backing up your data

Envision if the gadget on which you put away your business' monetary data was lost, hacked, or taken – and you did not have it upheld up anyplace. These problems can emerge whenever, and you should be set up to reestablish your books. Luckily, there are numerous reinforcement alternatives accessible that will empower you to keep an extra, state-of-the-art duplicate of the business financials.

6. Not using an accounting software

In case you're monitoring your business funds in an Excel bookkeeping page or a paper record, you might need to consider moving up to programming. Putting resources into the correct bookkeeping programming can assist you with maintaining a strategic distance from botches and, at last, make it simpler to deal with your accounts.

Most bookkeeping programmings incorporate the financial balance, meaning less manual work. These projects likewise make it simple to back up your information if there should be an occurrence of a crisis. Also, if you wind up expecting to recruit a bookkeeping administration for your business, having unified programming will guarantee the bookkeeper has all the recorded information they require to deal with your books, finance, and assessments.

Regardless of whether you're taking care of your bookkeeping or moving to an expert, accounting mix-ups can cause significant issues for your business. It is ideal to forestall & face these problems.

Chapter: 6 Business Challenges & Solutions

Small enterprises experience a number of obstacles throughout their first few years of operation. Others are more challenging to resolve than others, and according to the U.S. Bureau of Labour Statistics, about 20% of small companies collapse during their first year. Fifty percent go under by the close of their fifth year, and that figure increases to 80 percent by the tenth year.

With so poor survival rates, it's clear to see why people are worried for their first few years of the company. In fact, though, many common market issues and problems are actually fixable. You can notice several moments when you need to take a step back, make an effort to understand the pressure points that you experience and re-think your plan.

Each small business faces some problems here, including some tactical tips about how to solve them.

1. Find the Customers
2. Increasing Brand Awareness
3. Designing Email List
4. Lead Generation
5. Delighting the Customers
6. Hiring Talented People

7. Managing Workflow
8. Financial Strategy
9. Scaling

1. Find Customers

This first one is not just an issue for small enterprises. Marketers of well-known firms such as Toyota, Apple, KFC, and McDonald's are not yet waiting for the leads to come in: Also, the largest, most popular firms have employees working tirelessly to attract new customers every single day.

Finding consumers may be especially challenging for small companies that are not well-known. It seems, for instance, like there are too many platforms you may choose to concentrate on. How do you decide what to prioritize and where money can be allocated?

How to solve it:

Seeking consumers begins by deciding who the target consumer is. It does not work for everyone to spray and pray – you need to ensure you distribute the message to the correct people.

By designing buyer personas, you will get a feel of what your potential buyers are like, what they are doing, and where they spend some time online.

It will significantly boost the market outcomes by producing very particular ones. When you have developed your buyer personas, you can start developing content and reaching out to your potential buyers in areas where they invest time online and with ads that appeal to them.

2. **Brand Awareness**

Customers can not purchase from you if they don't know who you are. Often it may seem like the largest brands of today seem to have sprung up from nowhere. When did it turn into a household name? Why did they continue to spread so quickly? Is it feasible for your organization to expand in the same way?

Of note, the hard work, mistakes, and rejections of each of these businesses existed behind the scenes. But there are tactics how you can begin right away to spread the word about your company and create a strong reputation.

How to solve it:

There are several approaches to increase brand awareness, but concentrate on three in this book about public relations, blogging & co-marketing.

- **Public Relations**

Public relations are less about competing for a place on a news site and more about concentrating your message on the consumer and discovering your location. I suggest reading First Round Capital's excellent research about what entrepreneurs and small companies often get wrong regarding public relations, which also provides some useful guidance about how to find out who reports the industry, develop relationships, and communicate with reporters.

- **Blogging**

Running a high-quality blog on a daily basis can also help you create brand recognition. A blog not only helps push traffic to your website and turn the traffic into leads, but that also helps you to build authority and confidence among your prospects in your industry. It will also assist you in the creation of an email list, which takes us to our next step.

- **C0-marketing**

Collaborating with another brand allows you to inherit some of their name and credibility while still producing brand evangelists outside of your immediate radius. It's an ideal opportunity to complement the organic marketing activities by acquiring a wide range of potential connections. More details about how to get acquainted with co-marketing can be found in our ebook.

3. **Designing Email List**

You must create confidence by being top-of-mind and continually delivering value to drive prospects down their buyer's path to finally becoming your client.

The first move is to link prospects to your email list.

As if creating an email list is not complicated enough, the typical marketing account degraded by 22.5 percent last year. That means you'll need to expand your email list by nearly a quarter just to hold it up to date, let alone develop it. Seeking opportunities to continuously introduce fresh, different email addresses to the lists is the task of the marketing staff.

Yet what many people term "making an email list" is simply purchasing an email list, and it is never a smart idea to purchase an email list. I repeat not a good idea. It is not only a waste of resources, but it'll also damage your email deliverability and I.P. credibility. If purchasing or renting email lists is your new plan, then it's time to rebuild and find appropriate ways to position certain tools.

How to solve it:

Develop opt-in email lists instead of purchasing or renting lists. Subscribers who willingly give you their email address so that you can send them updates make up an opt-in email list.

The process of opting in needs the accessibility of the website that catches their email address. This can be accomplished with a shape builder or other method to transform (more on that later).

Creating a market is the other part of the puzzle. Through making excellent blog posts, you will do this and make it convenient for people to subscribe, which can help you improve your web visibility, build up search credibility, and develop evangelists from your content at the same time.

Create an informative opt-in message and email it to your old list, inviting contacts to re-opt-in and pledging to delete any contacts that don't reply.

Rising your email list does not often mean growing your sales-qualified lead list, which leads me to my next stage.

4. **Lead Generation**

Lead generation is another concern most small companies share, namely, creating sufficient leads to maintain the sales staff satisfied.

However, the most critical goal of a marketing team is to produce high-quality leads in vast amounts. A decent lead generation engine transforms website users into future buyers and maintains a constant stream of sales leads flowing in as you sleep.

How to solve it:

To make the lead generation method function for your business, you must first increase the conversion rate of your current website. The most critical asset you have for converting opportunities into clients is your website. Look and question yourself from your website:

Do visitors specifically direct each of the webpages to take some action, or do they leave them uncertain what to do next?

Can you use a program, like HubSpot's free lead generation tool, that instantly pulls the inputs from your forms and brings them into your communication database?

For any single campaign that you manage, can you build custom landing pages?

Do you have CTAs for any of your blog posts for lead generation? (Have you got a blog at all?)

First, prioritize the most major blogs on your website. The homepage, "About" page, "Contact Us" page, and probably one or two of the most famous blog posts are usually the sites that pull in the bulk of visitors for most companies. Learn how to decide which sites to prioritize and how to customize them in this topic.

Then, utilizing conversion applications such as:

- Hello bars, hello
- Pop-up windows
- Diaposit-ins

Finally, free lead generation tools and applications for startups can be used. It is a huge obstacle in and of itself to afford ads in general, but it can be a game-changer to identify and incorporate the most effective free marketing methods.

5. **Delighting the Customers**

A perfect target is consumer loyalty, but much greater is customer delight. After all, the ones who purchase from you again, write expert opinions and accept case studies, and recommend you to others they trust, are delighted consumers.

You have to transcend standards and offer an unmatched service in order to gain true consumer delight such that your consumers become promoters of your brand.

How to solve it:

For your customer, it takes effort to begin solving in a fashion that converts them into crazed fans. Here are few moves that will bring you into the proper mindset:

- Realize why you were picked by your customers and what they want and need
- At the beginning of the commitment, set clear goals
- Deliver on certain requirements (and serve the wishes of your customers)
- Dream of innovative approaches to include unique extras that go beyond and above the call of duty.
- Continue to monitor consumer loyalty and allow changes.

6. **Hiring talented workers**

Without a great team who knows your mission and encourages your actions, none of the above will happen at large.

Hiring is one of the most challenging tasks for small companies, particularly when small corporate leaders are often under-resourced to start with. Hiring new hires is a huge deal and a difficult operation, and most businesses invest about 4,000 dollars per new hire on onboarding. Employee attrition can be very costly if you do not recruit properly.

Still, as Howard Bernstein, CEO of 2020 On-site Optometry, says, it is hard to recognize anything on your own. That's why it is crucial to identify and recruit the best people and others who are genuinely passionate about what you are doing.

How to solve it:

For a short-term recruiting approach, it is simple to send out a work description, screen candidates, and make a decision. However, owing to the high expenses of recruiting the incorrect employee, it's essential to dedicate a considerable amount of time to the hiring phase. When you may locate excellent workers, do not settle for decent staff, even though it takes more time. Good workers are what can drive the business to the next stage.

And when you build customer personas for your employers, for your career seekers, create nominee personas. For each new job you recruit for, the personas must be different, but they may share certain basic characteristics across the culture of the business.

Next, take care in drawing applicants to the name of your company and making them involved in knowing more. This would assist you in creating a recruitment pipeline that will have the same certainty in hiring as it does in revenue. Then translate certain opportunities into applicants.

7. Managing the Workflow

When you have the staff in position to make the magic possible, handling operations as you scale is the next obstacle. You want to make sure the staff has the procedures and resources they need to perform successful work fast.

Around the same moment, as a corporate owner, you will not be everywhere at once. So, how can you remain centered on the market but still ensuring that everybody in the organization gets everything they require?

How to solve it:

By providing opportunities for them to get suggestions, the only approach to diagnose the barriers the team encounters and improve productivity is to build ways to identify them. It is possible to do this via:

- Surveys on employee satisfaction
- Frequent discussions of immediate reports one-on-one
- Assuring the success of your direct reports Hold one-on-one conferences for their direct reports
- Occasionally, skip-level meetings are conducted.
- Asking regarding group risks and the things that cause them the most "pain" in their positions
- Seeking the similarities & the bottlenecks in the reviews you get

8. **Financial Strategy**

More capital (whether staff, resources or time) can ideally improve productivity and output. Providing all of the support you can to the staff is the first move in maintaining smooth operations.

In principle, it seems easy, but have you realized the caveat, everything. Can you? Unfortunately, corporate owners have revenue-based and margin-based spending constraints.

It becomes a struggle then to maximise productivity when operating under such limits, investing in the company without going overboard.

By making sound choices focused on strong financial planning, this is solved.

How to solve it:

Each business is going to be different, so by remaining in front of invoices and bookkeeping, you'll need to use business credit carefully, reduce expenses where possible, and control cash flow. You will be assisted by corporate accountants and investment planners who evaluate the financial condition and help you to make sound choices.

9. **Scaling**

According to Nick Rellas, Drizly's co-founder and CEO, "There's this balance of creating power efficiency early, versus doing just what you have to do to get it all completed."

This is a complicated one, especially because every scenario is different. This topic can be seen in any aspect of the industry, including product growth, promotion, and content design, recruiting, and so on.

Most business leaders, for instance, would drive production at all costs. However, if you develop your business too fast, you'll find yourself trying to recruit staff quickly. Since preparation requires time, this can overwhelm the more seasoned team members. And if you wouldn't adequately prepare your staff, it might backfire.

How to solve it:

There's no right solution here, sadly. "The scale can tip one way or the other based on where you are in your business' lifecycle," Rellas says, "although I do agree you need both at various times."

Not obsessing about every aspect, but obsessing about the correct specifics, is what it comes right down to. For example, obsessing over product excellence may be less relevant than obsessing over customer care. It is easier to set away your worries and introduce a product that is not flawless so it can be changed and enhanced at all times. After all, you will understand a lot more easily what's effective and what isn't until the goods are in possession of your consumers.

Chapter: 7 Key Accounting Terms

The following are some standard accounting terminology that any small business owner should be acquainted with:

1. GAAP (Generally Agreed Accounting Standards)
2. Cash basis accounting
3. Accrual basis accounting
4. Accounts payable
5. Accounts receivable

1. Generally Agreed Accounting Standards (GAAP)

GAAP is a series of standard accounting principles that most American corporations are expected to follow. These guidelines detail how to keep track of, calculate, and report on the company's assets to third parties.

2. Cash basis accounting

Cash basis accounting is one of the two most popular accounting techniques, as it involves recording revenue and expenditures where they are earned and charged. Small companies like this approach because it is easy, despite the fact that it can offer a false impression of your cash flow (e.g., if you receive payment for a bill the month after you issued it).

3. Accrual basis accounting

Accrual basis accounting is needed for companies with a turnover of more than $25 million. You must log revenue as you charge it, rather than when it is paid, which implies you might be paying taxes on the money you haven't even received. However, opposed to cash basis accounting, it offers a more reliable long-term perspective of the finances.

4. **Accounts payable**

Accounts payable contains all unpaid payments for goods and services that you owe to suppliers. To accurately forecast cash flow, these liabilities must be considered against the company's assets and income.

5. **Accounts receivable**

Any of the money owing to the company by its consumers or clients is paid for in the accounts receivable. These accounts are normally monitored by invoices, which specify payment conditions (e.g., within a specified number of days of receipt) so you know when to expect incoming funds.

Chapter: 8 Common Accounting Reports

As part of their financial accounting procedures, every business must learn how to prepare a few main financial reports. Outside participants, such as owners, suppliers, and creditors, can use these documents to record the business's profits and expenses.

8.1 Profit & Loss Statement

When it is time to file your company returns with the IRS, accountants and tax preparers would most certainly ask for a (P&L) statement, but you will still need to share it with lenders if you apply for financing. Your profit and loss statement (P&L) outlines profitability of your company by listing gross margin, profit, sales, cost of goods sold and other primary indicators over a specific time period (monthly, quarterly and annually).

Profit and Loss Statement Template

[Company Name]

[Street Address], [City, ST ZIP Code]
[Phone: 555-555-55555] [Fax: 123-123-123456]
[abc@example.com]

Profit & Loss Statement

For the Period Ended ____________________

Income	**$**	**$**
Sales	0000000	
Services	00000000	
Other Income	00000	
Total Income		**0000000**
Expenses		
Accounting	0000000	
Advertising	000000	
Assets Small	000000	
Bank Charges	000000	
Cost of Goods Sold	00000	
Total Expenses		**00000000**
Profit/Loss		**0000000**

8.2 Balance Sheet

Balance sheet is a "snapshot" of the company's financial condition at any specific point in time. It includes a summary of the company's capital, assets & liabilities, both of which may be used to assess the valuation of your company.

ACCOUNT FORMAT

BUSINESS CONSULTING COMPANY
BALANCE SHEET
As at Date________

Assets	$	Liabilities & Stockholders' equity	$
Current assets:		Liabilities:	
Cash		Notes payable	
Accounts receivable		Accounts payable	
Prepaid building rent		Salaries payable	
Unexpired insurance		Income tax payable	
Supplies		Unearned service revenue	
Total current assets		Total liabilities	
Non-current assets:		Stockholders' quity:	
Equipment		Capital stock	
Acc. Deal - Equipment		Retained earnings	
Total assets		Total Liabilities & Stockholders' equity	

8.2 Cash Flow Statement

A cash flow statement is a financial statement that records and categorises each actual cost and revenue line by line, helping you to maintain track of the company's financial operation. About any line item in the cash flow statement would be identified as an operation, investment, or financing task.

You will also be liable for making a stockholders' equity statement whether the business includes shareholders or partners with equity in the company. This declaration, which is part of your balance sheet, outlines all adjustments in the valuation of the stockholders' equity rights over time, normally from the beginning of the end of the year.

Example Corporation
Statement of Cash Flows

		All numbers in thousands
Operating Activities	**$**	**10,100**
Net Income from Operations	$	10,000
Add: Depreciation Expense	$	100
Investing Activities	**$**	**(500)**
Purchase of Equipment	$	(1,000)
Sale of used equipment	$	500
Financing Activities	**$**	**4,500**
Increase in Long Term Debt	$	2,500
Issuance of Stock	$	5,000
Dividends Paid	$	(3,000)
Net Change in Cash Flow	**$**	**14,100**

Chapter: 9 Taxation

Taxation is the method of enforcing or levying a tax on individuals and corporate companies through a government or the taxing authority. Taxation applies at all levels, from corporate tax (GST) to goods and services tax.

9.1 What is Taxation

The federal and state governments have a major influence on how taxes are set around the country. The state and federal governments have enacted numerous policy changes in recent years to streamline the taxation mechanism and maintain accountability in the region. The Goods and Services Tax (GST) was one such reform that eased the tax system relating to the selling and distribution of goods and services in the world.

9.2 Purposes of Taxation

In the nineteenth century, the common assumption was that taxation could be used solely to support the nation. Governments have used taxes for more than just fiscal reasons in the past, and they do so again today. The differentiation between wealth sharing, income inequality, and economic prosperity is a valuable way to look at the function of taxes, according to American economist Richard A. Musgrave. (Sometimes global growth or progress and foreign competition are identified as distinct priorities, but they can be absorbed under the other three in general.) The first target, resource distribution, is reinforced if tax policy does not intervene with economic allocations in the absence of a legitimate justification for intervention, such as the need to minimize emissions. The second aim, wage redistribution, is intended to reduce income and wealth inequality disparities. The aim of stabilization is to sustain high jobs and market stability, which is achieved by tax reform, monetary policy, government budget policy & debt management.

9.2 Classes of Taxes

Taxes have been categorized in different forms in the theory of public finance, based on who pays for them, who carries the ultimate responsibility of them, the degree to which the burden may be transferred, and other considerations. Taxes are more generally categorized as either direct or indirect, such as the income tax of the former category and the sales tax of the latter. The requirements for discriminating between direct and indirect taxes are contested by economists, and it is uncertain which group such taxes, such as property tax or corporate income tax, should fall under. A direct tax is generally said to be one that cannot be transferred from the individual to anyone else, although it can be an indirect tax.

1. Direct Taxes
2. Indirect Taxes

Now we learn about direct and Indirect Taxes

1. Direct Taxes

Direct taxes are mainly imposed on individual citizens and are generally dependent on the taxpayer's capacity to compensate as determined by revenue, spending, or net worth. The following is a list of the most popular forms of direct taxes.

Individual income taxes are usually based on the taxpayer's gross personal net income (that might be an individual, couple, or family) that reaches a specified level. The conditions surrounding the capacity to pay, such as marital status, amount and age of the child, and financial pressures arising from sickness, are more widely tailored to take into consideration. Taxes are often charged at phased scales, which ensures that rates rise as income increases. A taxpayer's and family's personal exemptions can produce a range of income that is entitled to a zero-tax rate.

Net worth taxes are imposed on a person's overall net worth, which is proportional to value of assets less his liabilities. As in income tax, the taxpayer's specific situation should be taken into account.

Personal or direct consumption taxes (also referred to as taxes on spending or taxes on expenditure) are essentially imposed on all receipts that are not channeled into savings. In comparison to indirect spending taxes like the sales tax, a direct consumption tax may be customized to a person's financial circumstance by taking into account considerations like age, marital status, family status, and so on. This tax method has been implemented in only two nations, India & Sri Lanka, although it has long been appealing to theorists; both cases were short and ineffective. The "flat tax," which produces economic results close to those of the direct consumption tax by exempting many capital gains, came to be regarded favorably by tax analysts at the end of the 20th century. No nation has introduced a flat-rate tax base, while many have just one rate of income tax.

Inheritance taxation, in which the taxable object is the bequest earned by the individual inheriting, and estate taxes, of which the taxable object is the cumulative estate inherited by the deceased, are the two kinds of taxes imposed upon death. Inheritance taxes also take into account the taxpayer's specific conditions, such as the connection of the taxpayer to the beneficiary and his net wealth when the bequest is received. Estate payments, on the other hand, are normally phased depending on the value of the estate, although in certain nations, they include tax-free transfers to the partner and account for the number of heirs. Tax regimes which include a tax on gifts in excess of a certain threshold rendered by living individuals in order to avoid death duty from being circumvented by an exchange of property prior to death (see gift tax). Transfer taxes usually do not raise any money, if only because substantial tax collections can be prevented conveniently by estate planning.

2. **Indirect Taxes**

Indirect taxes, including imports and exports, are imposed on the output or sale of products and services or on transactions. Examples include general and limited excise taxes, VAT, taxes on some aspect of production or manufacturing, taxes on lawful purchases, and customs or import duties.

General sales taxes are levies that cover a large amount of consumer spending. The same tax rate may be extended to all taxable items, or separate rates can be applied to different products (such as food or clothing). Single-stage taxation may be levied at the retail level, like some states in the United States do, or at a pre-retail level (such as production or wholesale), as some developed countries do. At each point in the production-distribution process, multistage taxes are introduced. VAT, which grew in prominence during the second half of the 20th century, is usually collected by enabling the taxpayer to exclude from the sales debt the tax credit charged on transactions. At each point of the manufacturing and delivery process, the VAT has effectively substituted the turnover levy-a tax, with no tax relief charged at previous levels. Tax cascading, or the combined impact of the turnover tax, distorts economic decisions.

While they are usually applicable on a wide variety of items, sales taxes often exclude low-income families from the obligation to lower their tax burden. Excises, by contrast, are imposed only on individual products or facilities. Although almost all, including basics such as beef, flour, and salt, to non-essentials such as food, beer, cigarettes, coffee, and tea, to luxuries such as jewels and furs, taxes on a small category of goods, tobacco items, motor fuel, and alcoholic drinks, place excises and customs duties on most nations. Taxes on customer durables were extended on luxury items such as carriages, saddle horses, pianos, and billiard tables in earlier centuries. The car is currently a primary luxury tax item, primarily because registration regulations promote tax administration. Any nations also tax gaming & state-run jackpots have similar consequences as excises, with "take" of the government being, in essence, a gambling tax. Taxes on raw products, intermediate commodities (e.g., natural oil, alcohol), and equipment are imposed by certain nations.

Some excise duties and customs duties are particular, i.e., they are assessed on the grounds of the quantity, weight, duration, volume, or other particular features of the taxable product or service. Such excerpts, such as income taxes, are ad valorem, as determined by the price, depending on the valuation of the item. Legal transaction taxes are charged on the issue of bonds, on the selling (or transfer) of houses and land, and on sales on the stock market. They sometimes take the form of stamp duties for administrative reasons; that is, the legal or commercial paper is stamped to signify payment of the fee. Stamp taxes are regarded as an annoyance tax by many tax analysts; they are more often seen in less-developed countries & slow down the transactions on which they are applicable.

Chapter: 10 Small Business Tax Return

Most people are dreaming of holiday shopping, celebrations, and holidays as the year draws to an end. You're already worried about your 2017 tax return as a small business owner. Filing taxes, mostly as a small company, can be perplexing, daunting, and even cause you want to rip your hair out. It won't be too terrible if you take your time to make sure you have everything you need. Here's a short guide to filing a small business tax return in five easy measures.

1. Determine how to file
2. Collect all the documents
3. Find what forms you need
4. Make sure you are getting the deductions you deserve
5. Recheck your work with the help of a CPA

1. Determine how to file

The first step in planning for tax season as a small business owner is to know what sort of business you have. It would have an effect on the way you prepare your taxes. Are you a single proprietorship, an LLC, an S company, a general partnership, or a C corporation? When setting up your company, this should have already been known, but now it comes into play again. Different company forms have various criteria for tax returns, so it is necessary to consider what sort of business you are in order to understand what would be needed.

2. Collect all the documents

You've already learned that filing taxes needs a bunch of documentation, and this is true. Your documentation can be made up of real documents, or the documents might be digital. In any scenario, be-ensure you have them.

"The IRS says, "The company with which you are affects the kind of documents you need to maintain for federal tax purposes when it comes to what sort of documentation you can obtain. A list of your company activities should be included in your recordkeeping method.

Payroll, sales slips, bank slips, bounced checks, invoices, certificates, and cash register recordings are also exampling documents. Don't forget to keep track of travel costs, any sales, and records of items you buy and are using in your company, such as furniture or machinery. Last but not least, job documents are needed. Do the utmost to maintain track of these items during the year, instead of struggling throughout the tax season, to make it easy on yourself.

3. Find what forms you need

It's an unfair fact that while filing the taxes, there would be some filling-out of paperwork. The kind of small company you have may influence the forms to fill out, as described earlier. Every state may have its own types and specifications, so here's a short rundown on some of the federal income tax measures:

Form 1120 U.S. Business Income Tax Return-Form 1120 is for tax reports submitted by C companies. C businesses are organizations where the shareholders do not incur taxes on individual reports themselves.

Form 1120 S U.S. Income Tax Return – For S Companies, this is the form to use. S Company owners, unlike C Companies, pay income tax on their corporate income tax reports. As a consequence, each shareholder is expected to complete a Schedule K-1 Method.

Form 1065 U.S. Relationship Benefit Tax- You would need to plan one of these types if your small corporation is set up as a collaboration. Since partnerships do not incur income tax, this type is just for information purposes. Every participant may also need to fill out a Schedule K-1 Form if you are part of a relationship, which goes into specifics regarding the profits, dividends, and losses of each particular partner.

Form 1099 MISC-This is a form that is processed and issued as part of the tax return to any independent contractors you might have employed, and it is often submitted to the IRS.

You may still need to complete separate documents for the boss, such as Form W-2 Pay and Tax Declaration.

4. **Make sure you are getting the deductions you deserve**

Deductions are the one aspect of paying the taxes that may be deemed pleasant.

Taxes are not all about the government having its due, Drew Hendricks of Forbes points out. Some tax laws are loopholes that provide for deductions – which are simply opportunities for the government to get you and your company to use money the way it wants."

You have put in a lot of time this year because operating a small company is an expensive activity. Making the best of the tax deductions, but be mindful of what is and is not an appropriate deduction. The Internal Revenue Service (IRS) offers certain basic guidance in this regard. The deductible business cost must be "usual and essential." Supplies, car costs, corporate transport, contract labor, staff compensation, pensions, employee benefits, and employee investment systems are some of the most typical ones on a small business tax return. Be vigilant not to combine personal expenditures with work expenses and be mindful of what company costs are 100% deductible versus a lower percentage.

5. **Recheck your work with the help of a CPA**

It may be confusing to submit a tax return as a private citizen, and filing as a small businessman is much, much harder. It's important to consider the measures involved in processing a small business tax return, as well as the criteria. It is advised, however, that you enlist the assistance of a licensed CPA to ensure that everything is properly and accurately filled out, particularly if this is your first filing as a small business. A CPA will help you manage all the forms, locate deductions, and advise you what reports and documentation to gather are required.

Chapter: 11 How to Audit Your E-commerce Business

E-commerce is one of the fastest-growing business markets nowadays, so make sure you are prepared with an online business audit to help you develop the site. To boost traffic, make profits, and create a long-term consumer community, e-commerce companies need great material.

- How is the content performing?
- Is there anything that you should be doing?
- What was the last period you performed a comprehensive e-commerce audit?

It is important to take a step back and audit the material on a daily basis and ensure that it is fulfilling your company objectives. Continue reading to learn how to audit (and improve) your e-commerce material.

11.1 Review your current vision

Before you start your e-commerce business audit, you can do some deep thinking. This involves having a good, hard look at the new plan and finding some places that you might be falling short.

Do you really have any editorial calendar for the company's site and social network, for example? An editorial calendar is an important and basic function that many e-commerce company owners ignore.

- Take into consideration if the material is advertised. Are you making the best out of your email & social network accounts?
- Do the landing pages have well-defined objectives?

Prior to implementing some modifications or improving your approach after an e-commerce market analysis, you must first recognize existing issue areas that need to be resolved. You are already mindful of where (and why) you've been deficient in strategic guidance. Tackle certain places with passion, and bid farewell to your strategy-poor past.

11.2 Be critical

Now it's time to get back to work for the content auditing.

Create a list of every website on the e-commerce platform, beginning with the home & landing pages and making your way down to specific blog posts and product pages. Now go to each page and ask yourself the following questions:

- Is the website producing as it promises? Are your headings in line with your text? Do the call-to-actions execute on their promises?
- Is anything current? Since search engines don't value old material as much, it's crucial that the connections, items, and material are accurate and up-to-date.
- Is there a conceptual framework for each piece? Examine the organization on the website. It should sound normal and not haphazardly placed together.

- Is it easy to find? Internal links should be plentiful in your material, linking it all together. It's not just SEO-friendly, but it's still user-friendly.

- Is it efficient? Using the site analytics to see if any specific piece of material gets a tonne of traffic or converts. Don't forget these metrics if you want to expand your e-commerce business.

When undertaking an e-commerce company audit, don't be delicate with yourself: a stern eye on each material feature can sound harsh, but it will deliver the best outcomes.

11.3 Use tools to source the accurate data you need

Since an e-commerce company audit involves effort and time, it's a smart idea to use one of the numerous free or low-cost tools available to assist you to organize and quantify data easily. You have access to a wide variety of content resources, each of which is customized to a particular target.

- **Google Analytics:**

Google Analytics is helpful for finding issue areas and assessing the success of content by indicators.

- **Screaming Frog:**

Screaming Frog is an SEO tool that crawls your site and returns valuable (and actionable) details.

- **Site Analyzer:**

Site Analyzer offers a thorough review of the site, as well as an overall rating dependent on criteria such as speed, style, and copy.

- **Yoast:**

Yoast, a wonderful WordPress SEO plugin that offers a fast rundown of keyword targeting for blog posts and websites.

But be careful: with so many auditing tools at your hands, it's possible to get too dependent on them. To get the best out of the e-commerce quality audit, invest just in a handful and use them wisely. Don't get paralyzed by research paralysis. There are many resources that will assist you.

11.4 Get into auditing to maximize the value of your business

Finally, don't feel too cozy. Auditing is a constant phase that necessitates daily focus. Your content isn't a stand-alone entity; it's up against a slew of other products in a saturated sector, and standing away requires effort.

A content audit is a valuable practice that will help you keep on top of things. It's also a particularly rewarding talent to practice. Flipping websites is a popular route for aspiring entrepreneurs, and a content audit will make it simple for you to acquire an online company, transform it around, and then market it for a profit – it's a talent that can pay off again and again. It all comes down to providing outstanding web content in terms of profitability, performance, and market resale value.

Chapter: 12 The impact of Covid-19 on eCommerce

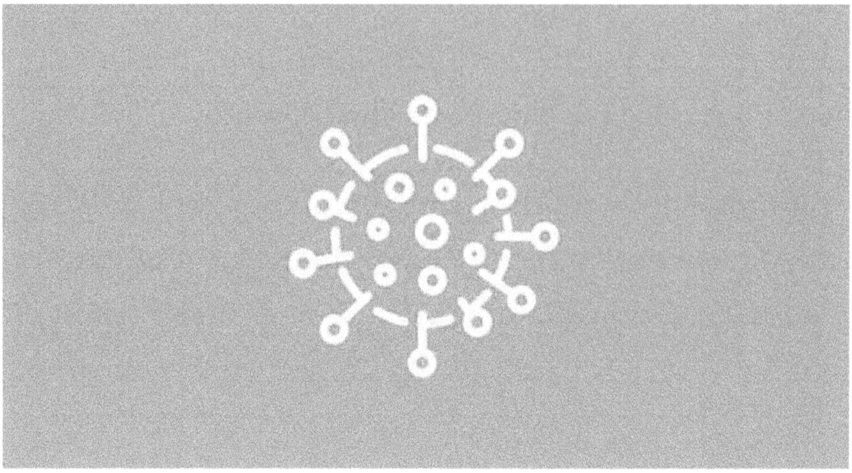

2020 was a difficult year for almost all individuals. Simultaneously, the online business developed more than ever. What would we be able to anticipate from 2021? SearchNode distributed another report on the most recent web-based business patterns and the effect of Covid-19.

A year ago, SearchNode distributed a report on online business patterns in 2020. Obviously, in those days, there was mostly secret about the Covid that would spread all over the globe. In the overview, there were loads of discussions with Magento, an improved spotlight on personalization and natural manageability.

2020 was, of course, all about Covid-19.

What has changed in a year? You should discover, as the Lithuanian tech organization distributed another report on online business patterns. In October 2020, the organization interrogated 100 internet business leaders from Europe and North America.

12.1 Six% eCommerce revenue decreased during the lockdown

There were inquiries concerning Covid-19. It appears to be that most web-based business organizations saw their online income increment during the worldwide lockdown in the spring of 2020. As per the study, 90% of organizations saw their online deals increment at any rate a piece, with 50% of respondents asserting it developed by more than 100%. Yet, 6% say their online business income diminished during Covid lockdown.

After the lockdown was finished, numerous purchasers began shopping at physical retailers once more. 86% of respondents say that their online incomes expanded, and just 4% say it diminished.

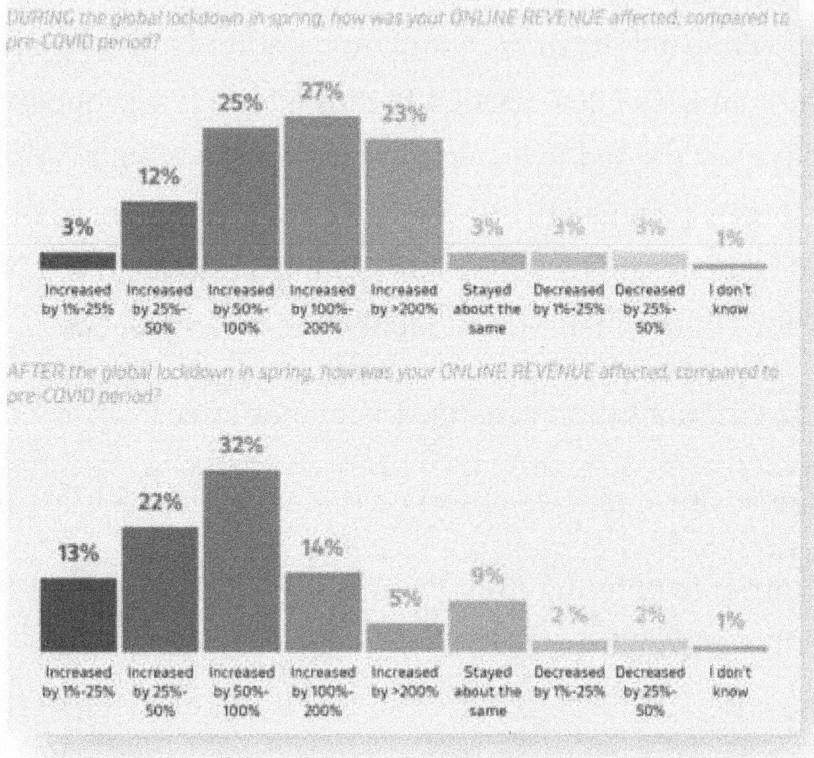

12.2 Online profit margin increased by 38%

Producing on the web deals is a certain something; the entire Covid-19 circumstance has additionally prompted things like disturbed inventory chains, inadequately staffed client assistance, and the sky is the limit from there. This straightforwardly influences the online net revenue. It appears to be that for 38% of internet business leaders, their online net revenue developed during the worldwide lockdown, while for a comparative rate (40%), the circumstance expressed about the equivalent. Just 15% asserted that it diminished.

12.3 The impact of Covid-19 on the workforce

The pandemic has, obviously, additionally prompted a few changes in organizations' labor force. Around 44% said they needed to move staff, while three out of ten recruited more individuals. The opposite side of the coin is that 26% needed to terminate a few groups, and 15 percent say they needed to lessen their workers' pay rates. Also, perhaps somewhat amazing for a few, yet 5 percent figured out how to expand compensations. What's more, much astonishing: 21% of organizations didn't change their labor force by any means.

21% of organizations didn't change their labor force.

23% of omnichannel players observed disconnected deals increment

Another intriguing finding from the investigation is that for retailers on the offline and online stores, 23% say their disconnected deals expanded, and 16 percent figured out how to keep it comparative. Lamentably, for 43%, their disconnected deals endured a shot.

12.4 Measurements for physical retailers

Numerous physical retailers needed to change their business on the off chance that they needed to maintain a strategic distance from to leave the business. In this way, numerous new practices were presented a year ago. Among the members, 31% presented in-store pickup, while 26% decided to present home conveyance. Sadly, around one of every five needed to close down some actual stores for great.

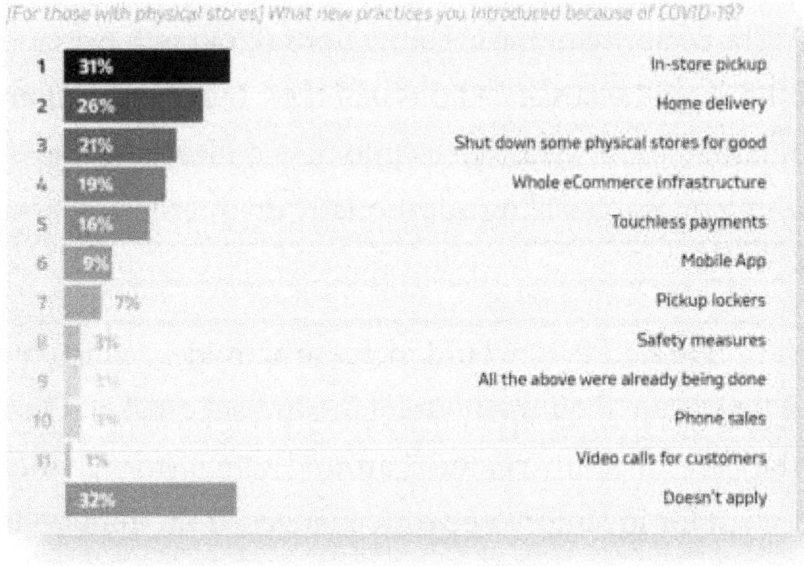

Covid has vigorously affected online retailers on various levels. Among the fundamental difficulties for internet business organizations, upset stockpile chains and satisfying interest for items were the, for the most part, referenced ones. Yet, restricted tasks because of the lockdown, overseeing stock, and the general absence of representatives were likewise vital difficulties for online retailers.

What's more, 17% said it was testing since they need to shut down their actual stores.

An upset store network was the primary test for some online retailers in Europe.

12.5 Shifted strategies

A year ago, numerous respondents said they would generally execute, improve or change personalization, site-search and omnichannel. This year, the essential vision has moved because of Covid-19. The majority of the organizations (45%) will presently have more spotlight on the advanced piece of their business by changing the combination, putting resources into new online business programming or emphasizing additionally on internet advertising channels.

One of every five said they would increase activities, which means they need to execute their methodologies and act quicker. One out of ten says they are currently centered around actual store changes, and 8 percent went for inventory network changes, from minor ones to new store networks or coordination's.

12.6 Financial consequences

Notwithstanding all the terrible things occurring because of the flare-up of the Covid, monetarily 2020 wasn't so awful for some web-based business organizations. The greater part of them (63%) say the year (up to October) was effective. Furthermore, 28% case their web-based business was progressing nicely, while their actual stores didn't. What's more, an astounding 2% said the inverse!

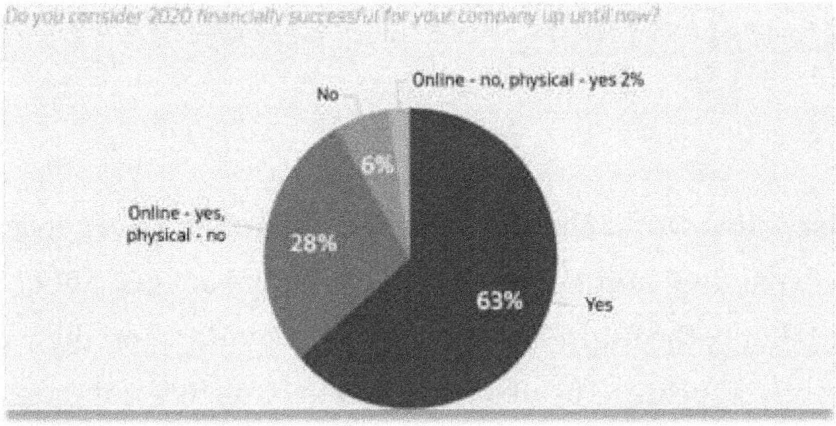
Do you consider 2020 financially successful for your company up until now?
No
Online - no, physical - yes 2%
6%
Online - yes, physical - no
28%
63%
Yes

Chapter: 13 What is the Future for Online Business?

With the online world changing apparently from one day to another and an expanding number of sites (today, there are just about 2 billion sites out there), the future for organizations working on the web consistently appears to be unsure. From the finish of unhindered internet to the limitations on YouTube adaptation to progressing computerized innovation and that's just the beginning, the inquiry is the thing that patterns will be generally noticeable for online organizations within a reasonable time-frame.

Right now, with the US economy extending, it appears to be that the not-so-distant future for online organizations is splendid gratitude to more noteworthy customer certainty and ways of managing money. What follows are new patterns in online business that have all the earmarks of growing as buyer propensities change over the following, not many years, which will significantly affect how web-based advertising is being performed.

Expansion of Cryptocurrency

While there has been impressive information about the inconveniences related to bitcoin, digital money itself has all the earmarks of being extending quickly and turning out to be standard. With more organizations and governments going to cryptographic money as an alternative, the exchanges will turn out to be solidly advanced. This implies an adjustment in the manner purchasers purchase across all business sectors, which implies that online organizations should be set up to acknowledge this type of cash soon.

The advent of Machine Learning

This type of innovation is ready to venture into deals and client service, implying that how organizations work with clients will be improved. AI will be through utilizing discourse examination, which better aids client assistance divisions in how to react to every one of their clients. This improves connection which means assembling a more grounded brand and enduring fewer misfortunes because of mistaken assumptions.

Increased Security Spending

In light of ongoing hacks and break-ins that have uncovered the individual data of millions of clients, more organizations are venturing up their security conventions to keep it from happening to them. This has implied a move in accentuation from avoidance towards recognizing interruptions and reacting in like manner. Better security implies more costs, which may tremendously affect the monetary situation of little and medium-sized online organizations.

Personalized Marketing

With such countless online organizations attempting to arrive at similar clients, it can get hard to get over the clamor. This is why individual promoting patterns have been developing and will keep on extending as more organizations spring up around the planet. Effective online organizations will zero in on brilliant showcasing that arrives at the individual, not simply the ideal buyer gathering. On account of new advanced innovation, specific Artificial Intelligence (AI) (web-based business organizations are now confronting this test), the progressions are now occurring and will keep on developing.

Rise of the Sharing Economy

The blend of the sharing economy, which is most broadly addressed by ride-sharing administrations like Uber. It has additionally dug into retail with monsters, for example, Google and Amazon getting into this pattern. For online organizations, the sharing economy addresses an incredible pattern ready to attack medical care and monetary administrations, which may change how numerous online organizations work.

For online entrepreneurs, the extension of the web to world business sectors implies a new wilderness of clients just as contenders. The individuals who succeed will be adaptable to the inescapable change that happens and finds a way to remain one stride ahead to guarantee their future.

Conclusion

Accounting is described as "the processing, review, and systematic documentation of numerical business transactions, the preparation of financial reports, and the examination and evaluation of these reports for management's knowledge and guidance."

Accounting is an accounting mechanism that observes, tracks, and communicates an economic entity's monetary activities.

It is the method of defining, evaluating, and communicating economic data in order for consumers of the data to make educated choices and decisions. Human life is evolving in this ever-changing environment.

Accounting has taken on a different form as a consequence of technical advances, such as holding records mechanically.

With the widespread usage of electronic accounting tasks, a modern arena has arisen. As a consequence, it is obvious that the concept of accounting will evolve in the coming years.

Bookkeeping and QuickBooks Made Easy

A Comprehensive Guide of 87 Useful Tricks to Hack QuickBooks and Organize Bookkeeping as a Silicon Valley Company

By

NESPY ONLINE MARKETING

Table of Contents

Introduction

This book is your basic guide to bookkeeping and QuickBooks. If you are a bookkeeper and want to upgrade your skillset and learn more about the QuickBooks software, this book is just for you. You will find a comprehensive detail of all the considerations, the advantages, and the ways you can become a QuickBooks bookkeeper. If you are a beginner and managing finances interests you, you can equally benefit from this book.

In the following chapters, you will find a detailed explanation of bookkeeping and why proper bookkeeping is necessary to keep businesses afloat. With people starting their businesses by the minute, the need for accurate bookkeeping is ever in demand. Small business owners invest in good financial handling software and outsourcing their account management to bookkeepers as affording an accountant is sometimes not possible for a small business owner.

You might question that bookkeeping is not as lucrative but do not pay head to that. Yes, conventional bookkeeping is becoming outdated, but still, there is demand. Most small business owners in the US use the software QuickBooks for their financial recording. Though some business owners know how to use it and keep updated, most of them will require help with crunching numbers and outsource professional bookkeepers to do the job.

QuickBooks was launched in the year 2003 by the company Intuit. After its launch, the company has launched various versions of the software to cater to different business owners' requirements. QuickBooks usage dominates the small business market by 80%. The company provides desktop-based and cloud-based versions of the software. From 2014 onwards there is a shift in trend. Before 2014, the business owners preferred the desktop model, but after the year 2014, more and more business owners are shifting to the cloud-based versions.

A whole chapter is dedicated to explaining the QuickBooks software. We discuss in detail the entire software. The services it provides and how a small business owner can benefit from it. There is a step-by-step guide to set up and install QuickBooks into your computer or other devices. After installation, guidelines are given to set up your account and add the vendor and customer accounts. A detailed explanation about how to enter employee details and how some versions can also manage automated payroll tasks. Reading about all this will make you understand the software's entire system and objective and realize how easy it is to operate. Technology has made even the most difficult and complicated tasks simpler for us. Now, it is our job to use technology for our benefit.

After you have understood the basic functioning of the software, you might want to invest in one. But this is not as easy as just purchasing one online. There are different packages of software available for different individuals. There are four basic packages available:

- QuickBooks Online
- QuickBooks Self-Employed
- QuickBooks Desktop
- QuickBooks App

Choosing the correct package that suits your requirements is also an important and difficult decision. In this book, we give you an overview of all the available packages and their specific features. All this information will hopefully make your decision easy.

In the US, the small to mid-size business market is denominated by QuickBooks users, and the owners are always on the lookout for professional QuickBooks bookkeepers for the job. You do not have to do it full time; you can manage all the accounts as a side hustle because QuickBooks software makes everything easy. You have to setup your accounting needs in the software, and most of the work is done by the software. However, it is n0t as easy as it sounds. The software is user-friendly, but you still require basic accounting knowledge and correct usage of the program. You might consider becoming a certified QuickBooks bookkeeper.

In this book, we have also discussed how in 2021, QuickBooks bookkeepers who work online make good money. There is a whole chapter in which we discuss working part-time as a QuickBooks bookkeeper is becoming a high-paying job. The average income of a QuickBooks professional in the US is discussed along with the US's best cities where you can practice QuickBooks bookkeeping. The considerations you should keep in mind while moving base to become a bookkeeper. California is the best place to be because the money QuickBooks bookkeepers are making there is approximately $10000 more than the US average per year.

There is an entire chapter dedicated to the ways you can become a certified QuickBooks bookkeeper. Sometimes a person knows what he/she wants but is unable to do anything because of the lack of guidance. This book gives you just that, proper step-by-step guidance on how to qualify yourself to become a QuickBooks bookkeeper. It does take time and effort, but you have numerous possibilities and options once you are qualified. To become a bookkeeper, you will need a certification. There are commonly three types of certifications you can choose from:

- QuickBooks Online Certification: Basic
- QuickBooks Desktop Certification: Basic
- QuickBooks Desktop Certification: Advance

The certifications are not just a one-time feat. You must keep your certifications up to date. You will require recertification each year by taking the certification exam. These tests are expensive but worth it.

Finally, we discuss the tricks and hacks you can use to use QuickBooks efficiently and effectively. These trips and hacks make your work easier and quicker. You will have to put in fewer hours. It is always wise to use trips and hacks and make the most benefit of the latest technologies. Sometimes doing online courses and certifications enable you to learn these tricks and hacks. Therefore, it is always recommended to keep your knowledge latest and keep improving your skills. The process of learning never stops. You keep learning throughout life. In present times learning has become a necessity rather than a luxury. In the ever-changing world, you will be left behind if you do not keep your skillset updated.

We hope you are going to find this book informative and helpful for your future professional endeavors. If bookkeeping is your calling, you should pursue it. It is one of the most in-demand services in the small business and mid-size business sector.

Chapter 1. Bookkeeping

In this chapter, we will focus on the basics. We will discuss the concept of bookkeeping and how it is the one-stop solution to all your accounting needs. Before anything else, we will try to understand what bookkeeping is and its importance.

Bookkeeping is an essential part of financial management. Small business owners sometimes try to manage the bookkeeping themselves, which becomes a reason for their businesses to fail. People do not realize that bookkeeping is a full-time job. You cannot manage a business and run numbers simultaneously. For this purpose, it is always wise to hire professionals for your accounting and bookkeeping.

1.1. What is Bookkeeping?

You must have heard about the term accounting. Bookkeeping is just that; it is related to managing the accounts. This term is used for business. The management of the complete finances of a business is termed bookkeeping.

To be more specific, we say that bookkeeping involves recording all the financing situations of a business. Bookkeeping is about keeping a record of all financial transactions daily, the influx and efflux of cash, the Payroll, profits, loss, investments, return on investments, and all the decisions related to the business's finance aspect. Bookkeeping helps the business owners keep track of all the information regarding the financial transactions.

After learning about what bookkeeping is, one wonders how a business owner can do all that by themselves? Not all business owners are literate about managing their finances. So, how can a business owner manage their accounts and finances? The simple answer to this question is a bookkeeper.

1.2. Who is A bookkeeper?

Bookkeepers are professionals who are responsible for managing all the finances of a company. They keep the owners aware of their present financial situation, record all related financial data and the total transactions made.

Correct bookkeeping is important for the business owners as well as prospected investors as well. Bookkeeping information is beneficial for the government and financial institutions as well. It will give a clear overview of the economic impacts of that certain business. Big companies and individual investors tend to research before they invest their money somewhere. The best and most reliable source of this information can be found in the company books. Looking at the books, the investor will decide whether he/she wants to invest in a certain company or project. In this way, bookkeeping is important for the owners because it is like his business introduction to the investment world. The better and more accurate the bookkeeping, the more chances of investment.

(A typical Bookkeeper)

1.3. Importance of Bookkeeping

When people start a new business, they tend to neglect the importance of good bookkeeping. Finance must be taken charge from day one and cannot be neglected for a single day. Now, what does bookkeeping do? It gives the company a tangible indicator of its performance and current situation. With this information's help, it becomes easier for the owner to make proper decisions financially, revenue generated, the profits, the loss, the income goals, etc. Each transaction must be recorded; the cash influx, efflux, credits, assets, liabilities all need to be recorded.

Bookkeeping is essential to keep the business afloat. Bigger companies usually hire accountants for the financial department, but it is not always possible for small business owners. So, small business owners mostly rely on hiring a bookkeeper. There whole accounting companies from where you can outsource a bookkeeper. It is cheaper than employing a full-time accountant, and a bookkeeper can easily manage a small business account. Anyone who starts a new business should never ignore the importance of keeping a record of every dime they spent and earn. Everything should be recorded.

1.4. Type of Accounting Method

Each business model follows one of the two accounting methods.

- Cash Basis of Accounting
- Accrual Basis of Accounting

To implement the bookkeeping function properly, the business owner should decide which accounting method they will follow. There are two basic models for accounting which are mentioned above. Now, what is the difference between these two? We will try to explain:

Cash Basis of Accounting:

In this type of accounting, a transaction is only recorded when a payment or cash is received or spent.

For example, if you buy fifty units of a product and the payment will be done after two weeks. No transaction will be recorded. It will only be recorded after two weeks when the payment is made. This type of accounting model is now considered outdated in present times.

Accrual Basis of Accounting:

In accrual accounting, the expenses and revenue are put down when the transaction is made rather than when the payment is made.

We use the same example of buying 50 units of a product and payment must be made after two weeks. The record will be entered as soon as the receipt is received and will be recorded as payables. This is the more modern model for accounting and is widely accepted.

1.5. What do the bookkeepers do?

Now that you have a basic idea of who a bookkeeper is let us move to the set of responsibilities and jobs the Bookkeeper carries out. Listed are the tasks carried out by bookkeepers that make it convenient for the business owner to systematically run the business and provide a clear picture of its financial position. The responsibilities of bookkeepers include:

- Recording transactions every day.
- Sending invoices to clients.
- Keep track of payments.
- Prepare and maintain the payable ledger.
- Manage the cash flow.
- Compile and maintain all accounts.

1.5.1. Record the Transactions Each Day

One of the jobs of the Bookkeeper is to enter the transactions each day. These include bank transactions. Nowadays, most companies use software to manage accounts. Some software has a function to generate automated bank feeds, which makes the task easier. You must keep a check on the cash, and precious data entry time is saved.

1.5.2. Sending Invoices to Clients

Another responsibility of the Bookkeeper is to make receipts and invoices on purchases and send them to the clients.

1.5.3. Keep Track of Payments

Once the invoice is sent out, keeping a record of the payments received is also the Bookkeeper's responsibility. To keep a follow-up to receive pending payments is also the responsibility of the Bookkeeper. This is also known as being responsible for the receivable ledger.

1.5.4. Being Responsible for the Payable Ledger

Up to a certain amount determined by the business owner, the Bookkeeper makes the payments made on the owner's behalf. The Bookkeeper keeps records of all the payments made by the business. These include the payments to the suppliers, the extra cash available, and the other business expenses. The Bookkeeper records all this information and checks it every day.

1.5.5. Responsible for Managing the Cash Flow

One of the most important business rules is that a certain amount of cash is always available. The responsibility of the Bookkeeper is to always maintain the balance. This can be done by keeping a record of the day-to-day expenses and revenues. There should always be cash available for the day-to-day expenses. If the Bookkeeper suspects that the balance might be disrupted, he/she can offer advice to the owner by telling them ways to control the outflow and increase the inflow. These devices are almost always short-term fixes.

1.5.6. Compile All Accounts

The most important job of the Bookkeeper is to maintain the account books. The account records should all be up to date. These include all the ledgers. This is necessary for further investments and business decisions. The owner or prospect investor looks at these accounts and makes decisions according to the financial situations mentioned in the books.

1.6. How can a Bookkeeper be Beneficial for Business?

When you have a smaller business setup, it makes sense to manage your account yourself. But when the business expands, it is always a good idea to hire someone to take care of the bookkeeping. In this way, you can concentrate on expanding the business, and your Bookkeeper can take care of your day-to-day expenses. Many people do not hire a bookkeeper to save money but lose a lot of precious time in managing their account that they could be using to innovate and expand their business. Bookkeeping is a time-consuming job, and it should be left to the ones who are professionally trained to do so. They might as well do the job better and take less time. Following are listed a few benefits of hiring a bookkeeper:

1.6.1. Let you Focus on Your Business Strategy

As explained earlier, bookkeeping is a time-consuming task and demands attention to detail. Hiring a bookkeeper will save you all that time, and you will have plenty of time to focus on your business.

1.6.2. The Accounting Cost can be Saved.

If you have a small business, it is a better idea to hire a bookkeeper. If you hire an accountant, it will cost you more money and will become a liability. All the recording and accounts can be easily managed by a bookkeeper as well, and it will cost you a lot less money.

1.6.3. Double Check Your Cashflow

As a business owner, it is wise to always keep your eyes on the cashflow. But sometimes, you can get caught up, and in that situation, your Bookkeeper is there to tell you when you need to manage your cash flow. The Bookkeeper can warn your earlier, and you will still have time to manage the situation.

1.6.4. Be Informed of Current Financial Situation:

As the Bookkeeper is working on a day-to-day basis, he/she will be aware of all the business's financial situations. If you require any help and advice in this department, you can advise your Bookkeeper to have the complete information and explain the clear picture to you.

1.6.5. The Financial Data is Organized

In case you get hold of good software like QuickBooks, the Bookkeeper will work on the same software. The data is kept organized and transparent using the software because the margin for mistakes is highly reduced. The accountant can analyze the same data if you wish to get advice regarding business expansion and investment.

All in all, bookkeeping is particularly useful for business owners and investors alike. If you are not a businessperson and are interested in managing accounts for other small businesses, bookkeeping could be a good profession for you. The possibilities are limitless.

Chapter 2. QuickBooks Explained

With a basic knowledge of bookkeeping and what it means for small businesses, we can now discuss bookkeeping solutions. 2021 is all about solutions. Bookkeeping is a difficult task. It can be made easy with the help of accounting software. In this chapter, we are going to discuss software known as QuickBooks.

1.7. 2.1. What is QuickBooks?

If you are a small business owner and you aim to reach the next level, you might want to start keeping track of your finances. Most people control their finances when they start with a business, but it becomes difficult once the business gains pace. If you wish to expand your business, you will have to become more proactive, take hold of your finances, plan your next financial moves, keep an eye on day-to-day transactions, and organize a cash inflow and outflow system. You should set up a payroll. All the administrative work should be organized. Reading all this must have given you a headache. You were thinking about making some money; how are you going to manage all the financial stuff?

It would be best if you were thankful for your stars that you live in the 21st Century and there is software available for everything. In this chapter, we are discussing accounting software that works like magic. The software is known as QuickBooks. QuickBooks is the perfect tool for your financial necessities.

2.1.1. QuickBooks

It is accounting software that has features to organize the financial aspects of small businesses. The functions of QuickBooks include:

- Recording everyday transactions
- Track and record revenue and expense.
- Report generation for planning
- Prepare bills.
- Preparation of Payroll

The software is targeted towards small to medium-sized business setups. The QuickBooks software has features that make it possible for you to manage report generation, sales, cash flow, billing, revenue, taxes, reporting and expenses. The best part about the software is that there are inbuilt templates for reports that you can easily set and customize according to your specifications. It is easy to fill in data to an already prepared template compared to create by yourself. You can take control of your finances. It is a user-friendly software, but it has a learning curve, and you must have some basic accounting knowledge to operate and use this software. To use the software effectively, you must learn and have an in-depth knowledge of the software's essential functions.

2.1.2. The History of QuickBooks

In 1983, two inventors Scott Cook, and Tom Proulx, created the company Intuit. QuickBooks is a product of this company and was first launched in 2003 and targeted to small businesses. Over the years, better and more functional versions of the software have been launched. It remains one of the most widely used financial software for small businesses in the US. Different versions of the software are available in the international markets as well.

1.8. 2.2. QuickBooks Features

QuickBooks is amazing software with multiple features and functions. Here is a list of a few features of the software.

2.2.1. user Friendly

This software is super user-friendly. It is easy to use and navigate. All the financial features needed for a small to medium business are present in this one program. You do not have to record your data in different locations. This single software manages all your data.

2.2.2. Data Migration

This is a wonderful feature. If you want to transfer any data from QuickBooks to the spreadsheet, the transition is smooth. When there is a requirement to present the data on a spreadsheet, you can easily transfer all the software from the software without manually copying it.

2.2.3 Smooth Navigation

To use this software is easy because the navigation is simple. Everything is displayed clearly, and working is smooth. The program interface is clear and simple. However, you will have to learn and get used to the software before you can use it. You need to learn and understand all the financial terms and data entry methods to using this software effectively.

2.2.4. Smooth Transactions

The bank transactions are systematically recorded. Each entry you make is recorded. You can even set up regular transactions like salary payments, commissions, and bills repeated each month or every two weeks. These transactions will be automatically recorded.

2.2.5. Invoices

You can set up the invoices to be generated. The software can even generate invoices from your smartphone or tablet if they are installed with the software. You are not dependent on the computer system or laptop to generate business invoices. This feature is truly per the present requirement where everything can be achieved with a click of a button anytime, anywhere.

2.2.6. Calculate Tax

The feature of tax calculation is included in the software. To do taxes is always a tricky business. With the QuickBooks software, you can easily calculate the taxes quickly, efficiently, and accurately.

2.2.7. Projections

There is an automated feature in the software that will present you with projections. The software can generate all kinds of projections, including profits, expenses, sales etc. Getting the projections makes it easy to make financial decisions.

1.9. 2.3. Set-up QuickBooks

To use QuickBooks, you must have basic accounting knowledge and your own business. To use this software, you must be organized and willing to manage your finances seriously and as a daily feature. Some people install QuickBooks, put in the money, and forget it for months. Some purchase it and never even learn how to use it. QuickBooks does not work in that manner. You must be willing to learn and be consistent. Consistency is the key.

Let us discuss step-by-step guidelines for using QuickBooks.

2.3.1. Start

The first step will be to install the software properly. For installation, you must decide how you are going to use it. When you start the program, you will have two options:

- Network
- Custom Options

You will choose the Custom settings if you use the software on only one computer and use the same computer for installations.

In case more than one computer will use the software, chose the Network setting.

After that, choose the location or folder in your PC where you wish the software to be installed. Add your details, and then set up your company file. After that, click on the QuickBooks icon on the desktop.

2.3.2. setup

As soon as you click on the QuickBooks program, you will see an Easy Setup Wizard to help you set up your company file. By following the simple instructions, you can set up your company file. If you are new to this kind of software, you will be favorable to take help from the wizard. It will make the setup smooth and easy.

2.3.3. Vendor Setup

The next step will be setting up the accounts for your vendors. You will click the Vendor Center in the toolbar placed at the top. Next, select the New Vendor option, and create a vendor account. To add a new transaction, click the New Transaction and fill in the details. You can even bring in details from MS Excel and MS Word.

Add all the vendors similarly if you have more than one.

2.3.4. Setup Employee Accounts

To set up the employee accounts, click the Employee Center. Then click the New Employee button and then add the related information. After the information, you click the button for New Transaction. Add the salary details and any other transaction related to that specific employee. For salary, you must add the date and time for each month. For that, you will click Enter Time and then add the specific time and frequency of salary. Some employers pay per month, and some pay by the week. Put in the information accordingly.

2.3.5. Set Up Customer Account

Like the vendor and employee accounts, add the customer accounts. First, you go to the customer center, then Add Customer and Job. Here you can add it as an income source. Now add the related transaction by clicking New Transaction. Here you will add the information for payments and generation of invoices. There is a link for Excel as well as Word. You can bring the information from Excel and use Word to prepare letters for the customer.

2.3.6. Setup Report Generation

Next, you will go to the Report Center. All the information added by you can be viewed here. You can also customize the kind of report you want to generate. Reports for-profits, payments and expenses can be generated separately.

Add all the employees the same way if you have more than one.

1.10. 2.4. Using QuickBooks

After the set up let us try to understand the day-to-day working of the QuickBooks software. What should we expect from the software? How can we manage our finances? What is the essential feature of the software? All these questions will be answered in the following part of this book. Together we will try to understand how the QuickBooks software works.

2.4.1. Chart of Accounts

So, what can you find on the chart of accounts? It will display the company's income, liability, expense accounts, assets, and equity to assign day-to-day transactions. This is what you will find:

- All the financial information about the company. It has the balance sheets, dividend, savings, receivables, and expenses. All this can be seen in the Chart of Accounts as a list.
- All the accounts related to the business, along with the account balances and account numbers. The details of the account

holder will also be shared, like the full names and contact numbers. All these accounts will appear when you click the List Menu in the QuickBooks chart of accounts.

2.4.2. Other Lists

These include the list of vendors you deal with. All your regular customers and customer accounts are listed. All the items you deal with and their inventory is listed.

How this is favorable for the QuickBooks user:

- You can manage everything in one place. You do not have to manage multiple lists and settings. All information is compiled in one place. Either it is the product inventory or the vendor; all can be managed in one place.

- When you have all the information in a single space, you can move back and forth with all the lists, account details and information. You can simultaneously manage all your financial situations together. Everything is easy to navigate and extremely user-friendly.

- Another feature is the easy addition ad deletion of details. It is simple to add new accounts, and it is equally simple to delete accounts. Anytime you want to change the existing settings, it is easily done.

- Apart from adding ad deleting details, you can also edit details. Correction and updating details are easy in this software.

2.4.3. The Reports

Report templates are already included in the software so that you can customize them according to your needs. Add the details of your vendors, customers, and items. You must add dates and times as well.

Once you start adding details accordingly and you update daily transactions and activities. The reports will be forming themselves. Anytime you feel like having an overview of your business, you can pull out reports with just one click, and the reports will be generated. These reports will help you make important financial and investment decisions.

2.4.4. payroll

QuickBooks makes it easy to manage payrolls. With the software, you add the information, and the program will itself arrange the payroll process. The software can itself manage the accounts of the employees who have tax exemption. You can customize the settings for other incentives and deductions. If you turn on the setting, the software automatically sends emails, deposits, and receipts.

More than one person can manage the payrolls in this software, the one who has purchased the software has to allow the other users on the network by assigning permission.

1.11. 2.5. QuickBooks Versions

QuickBooks is available in different types and versions. Each has a different package and fee. The versions are discussed in detail in the following chapters. Here we will list down the various versions of QuickBooks software:

- QuickBooks Online

- QuickBooks Self Employed
- QuickBooks App
- QuickBooks Desktop Products
    - QuickBooks Pro
    - QuickBooks for Mac
    - QuickBooks Enterprise
    - QuickBooks Premier

Chapter 3. Choosing the Best Version of QuickBooks

With the knowledge you have gained in the previous chapters, you know that QuickBooks is a financial solutions software. It was launched 25 years ago, and it has been the top choice for financial management since 2003. If you look at the company profits, they will show you an upward trend for the last 11 years straight. In addition to that, QuickBooks is used by 80% of small business owners in the US. This information enough should convince you to invest in the software.

Once you have decided to purchase the QuickBooks software, you are faced with yet another dilemma. Which version is for you? As discussed in the previous chapter, various versions of QuickBooks are available.

The QuickBooks family has a product for everyone. Here is a quick assessment of what you may want to purchase.

- If you are self-employed, run your company alone, and are looking to invest in a cloud-based accounting system, you should invest in QuickBooks for Self-Employed.
- If you own a small business and are interested in a cloud-based accounting system, you should invest in QuickBooks Online.
- If you are a small to medium-sized business owner, you must invest in QuickBooks Desktop.

- If you are already using QuickBooks and wish to update to another version, invest in QuickBooks Apps.

One of the deciding factors in any investment is the price range and affordability. This is the approximate price of the QuickBooks Packages available, making it easy for you to decide which product is best for you and is easy on the pocket.

Version	Usage	Price
QuickBooks Online	For businesspersons who want flexible financial access. This is suitable for small to mid-size business owners.	$25 up to $150/month
QuickBooks for Desktop	Suitable for small to medium size business owners in any sector	$399.99 with a one-time payment to $1,213 for one year
QuickBooks for Self-Employed	This is suitable for individual property agents, independent vendors, and Uber workers.	$15/ month
QuickBooks Mac	This is for small to	$399.99 paid once

	mid-size businesspersons who have their business set up on MAC	

(Prices of Different Versions of QuickBooks)

1.12. 3.1. QuickBooks for Self-Employed

QuickBooks Self Employed is the newest addition to the QuickBooks software versions. This is cloud-based software for financial services. It is specially designed for self-employed business owners and freelance service providers. It is ideal for independent workers like Lyft and Uber drivers. Property agents can also use it.

As this is a cloud-based program, you can access it with any computer or device with the given login.

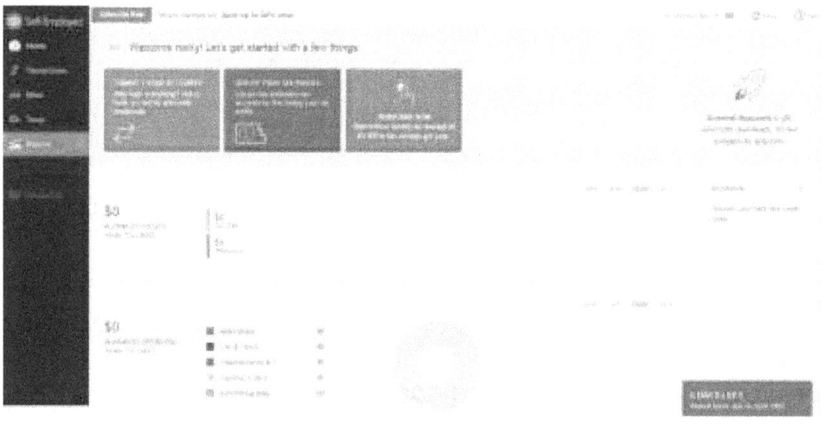

(QuickBooks Self Employed Interface)

(Display of Reports on QuickBooks Self Employed)

Using this program, you can send data to TurboTax and track personal and business expenses from a single bank account. It also calculates the Quarterly Tax and reminds you of payment.

You will find three types of packages available for QuickBooks for Self-Employed:

3.1.1. QuickBooks Self Employed Package

Investing in this package gives you the following features:

- Users can easily connect to their bank account through QuickBooks Self -Employed
- The users can also connect to their credit cards.
- Users can track the expenses and income from the same account but can be separated into personal and business groups.
- The software calculates taxes quarterly.

3.1.2. QuickBooks for Self-Employed Tax Bundle

This offers all the services provided by the simple package with an addition:

- Users can connect to Intuit Turbo Box that enables them to pay taxes online each quarter.

3.1.3. QuickBooks for Self-Employed Live Tax Bundle

Provides all the services as the packages mentioned above with an addition that:

- Users can consult a CPA all year round.
- The users can get the services of a CPA to review taxes.

3.1.4. Benefit

It can track traveling and Mileage. You can enter trips with dates, reasons, and distance traveled. The system will automatically calculate deductions.

3.1.5. Drawback

Does not provide a service to generate invoices and online payments.

1.13. 3.2. QuickBooks Online

QuickBooks Online is also a cloud-based financial solutions software. This had become exceedingly popular after 2014 when it was observed that more business owners preferred the online version over the desktop version. After that, the number of subscribers to the QuickBooks online version has been more than 1 million subscribers. This also tells us about the shift of business owners to a cloud-based system and shows their confidence in solely cloud-based software.

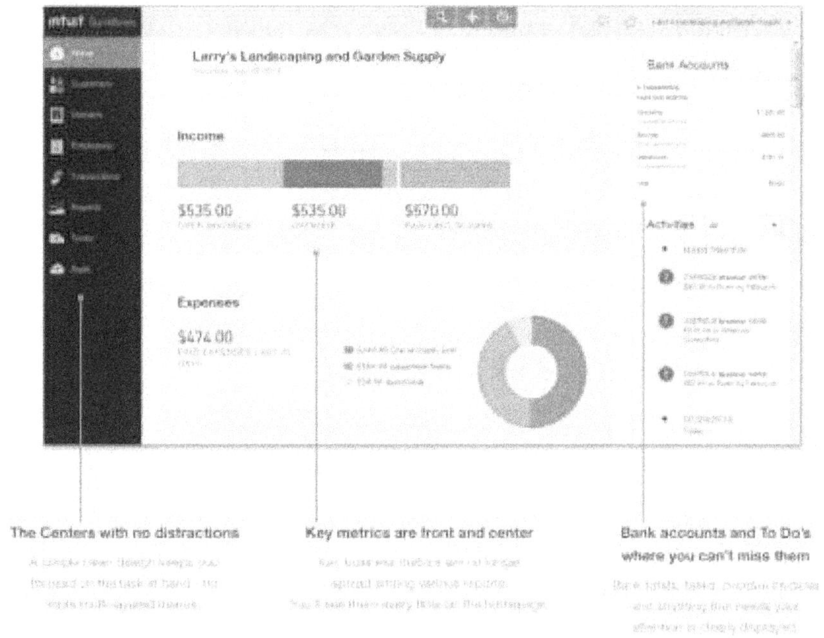

(QuickBooks Online Interface)

3.2.1. Common Features

The common features of QuickBooks Online are:

- Payable and Receivable Accounts:

The program can successfully manage expenses as well as income.

- Invoices and Bills:

It offers recurring or single-time invoices and can pay bills online.

- Management of Expenses:

The software can track all the business-related expenses.

- Reporting:

There are templates of prebuilt reports provided in the software, including the sales and tax reports. Simple Start gives 20 templates, Essentials gives 40 such templates, and gives 60 templates.

The QuickBooks online package does not need to be installed and comes in four packages:

3.2.2. QuickBooks Online Simple Start

The features provided in this package are:

- There is a single-user license.
- You can import your data from the QuickBooks Desktop version or MS Excel.
- You are entitled to consult two accounting professionals (bookkeepers and accountants)

3.2.3. QuickBooks Online Essentials

This version has all the abilities of the above version and, in addition to those capabilities, also has the following capabilities:

- The user is entitled to have 3 user licenses.
- The owner can set up user permissions to determine who is entitled to use the software.

3.2.4. QuickBooks Online Plus

All the capabilities of the Essentials version plus the following added qualities:

- Can set up 5 user licenses.
- The ability to track inventory.
- Users can create and send orders of purchase.

3.2.5. QuickBooks Online Advanced

This includes all the capabilities of the Plus version and the following capabilities:

- Can set up 25 user licenses.
- The ability for automated bill payment.
- The user can set up customized permissions.

3.2.6. Benefits

It is available for iOS, Windows, and Android devices. It can be connected to PayPal and Shopify for transactions.

3.2.7. Drawbacks

All the functions available in the QuickBooks Desktop are not available on QuickBooks Online. This version does not allow the addition of more than one company.

1.14. 3.3. QuickBooks Desktop

The QuickBooks Desktop is the most elaborated software version among all three of the versions. Most business owners prefer cloud-based financial services, but if you prefer desktop-oriented software, the QuickBooks Desktop version is for you. This version further has six more variations suitable for different types of small businesses. The six types are briefly explained as follows:

3.3.1. QuickBooks Desktop Pro:

This is good for most small businesses that are not involved in product manufacture.

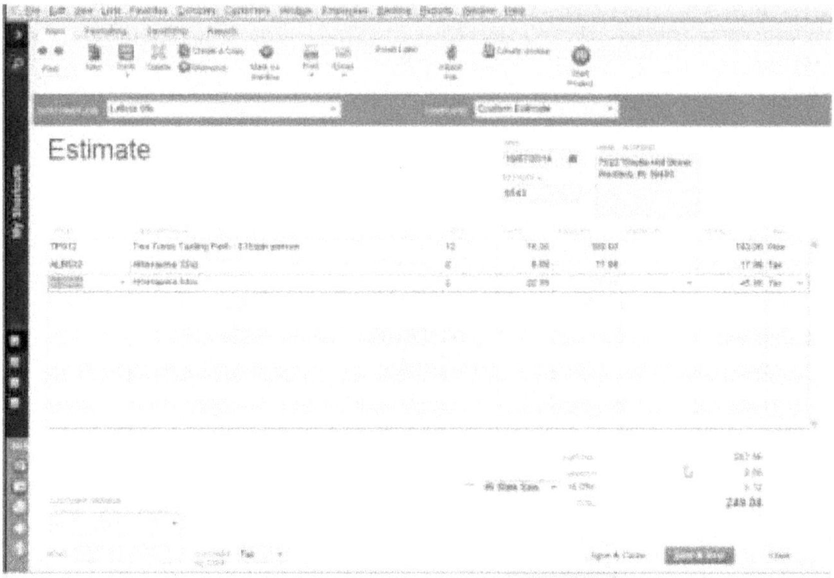

(QuickBooks Desktop Pro)

3.3.2. QuickBooks Desktop Premier:

This version is ideal for businesses involved in manufacturing, retail, and related to charity and non-profit organizations.

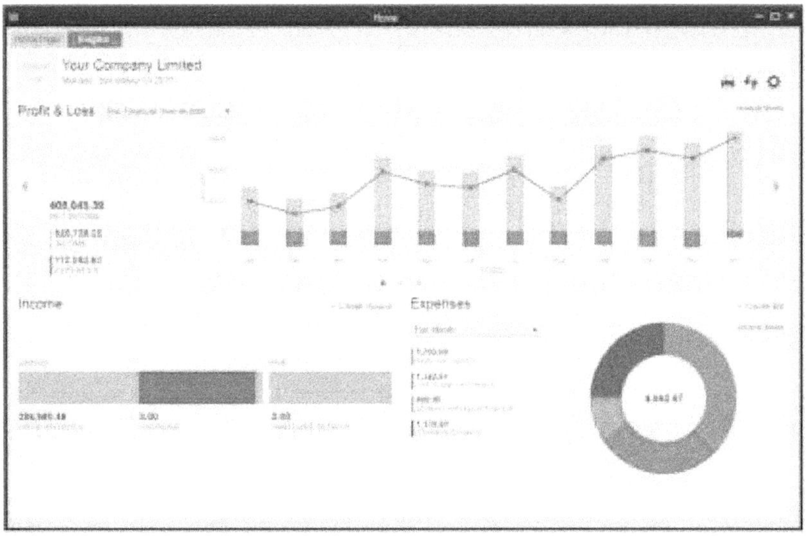

(Homepage of QuickBooks Desktop Premier)

3.3.3. QuickBooks Desktop Enterprise:

This is for large companies and enterprises. This version has industry reporting and a custom chart of accounts.

(QuickBooks Desktop Enterprise sales management)

3.3.4. QuickBooks Desktop Plus and QuickBooks Desktop Pro

The QuickBooks Desktop Plus and QuickBooks Desktop pro versions are sold as a yearly subscription rather than a one-time purchase. With these versions, your QuickBooks version is updated yearly, you are entitled to customer support, and your company data will be backed up.

3.3.5. QuickBooks for Mac

This is the only version compatible with Mac. It is like the QuickBooks Desktop Pro version. This is useful for most of the small businesses which are not involved in manufacturing.

1.15. 3.4. QuickBooks Apps

QuickBooks Apps are applications that can be used in combination with the QuickBooks software to enhance their features. These are also known as add-on applications. These add-ons can be purchased from the QuickBooks website. Some of the QuickBooks Apps are as follows:

3.4.1. QuickBooks Payments

This can be used as an add-on for the QuickBooks desktop to add some payment functions. This app enables the business to accept payments online as well as through credit cards. This also enables emailing of invoices.

3.4.2. QuickBooks Point of Sale

This is a cloud-based application. It enables the businesses to accept credit cards, track inventory and ring up sales through a point-of-sale dashboard.

3.4.3. QuickBooks Payroll

This app enables businesses to provide salaries to up to 50 employees by cash deposit or check. Two types of versions are available:

- Self-Service Solutions
- Full-Service Solutions

The app can calculate the state, federal, and local taxes automatically.

1.16. 3.5. Find the Best Version for You

QuickBooks has been a prominent player in the American market as a financial solution provider. The possibilities are numerous with this software. If you are a new business owner or plan to expand your business, QuickBooks will have a suitable version for you. But how to choose one which best suits your requirements? Here is a list of actions you can take before purchasing QuickBooks software. These activities will clear your dilemma, and the choice can be made easily:

3.5.1. Read Reviews

The best way to get a clear idea about a product is by reading reviews of people who have already used it. See which product is continually rated better. Read about the kind of services the software provides. Sometimes you get more knowledge about a product or service from reading someone's review. Always go through people's reviews and consider the products that most people are buying. Their performance must be the reason for their higher sales.

3.5.2. Take an Online Survey

When you are doing your research online, you may come across some online surveys which ask a few basic questions about your business and earnings. When you have entered your answers, the automated program will suggest the best software for you.

3.5.3. Talk to an Expert.

If you are still confused about which software to buy, try talking to an expert. A professional will be in a better position will suggest you according to your needs.

Chapter 4. The Best Way to Make Money In 2021

The year is all about small businesses and freelance work. In uncertain times everyone is pushing for a side hustle. We often have a misconception that the difficult part is setting up a business; other things follow once that part is covered. We cannot be more wrong in that approach. Though getting an idea, arranging for the finances, resources, place, and the raw material is tough and difficult to obtain, keeping the business afloat once launched is the trickier part. Most businesses come to an end, not because there is a lack of work, but because they could not manage the finances. Not all are indeed good at numbers and finance, and often, help is required.

People have now understood the importance of managing finances and are eager to outsource business financing. Here enters the role of bookkeepers and financial professionals. With the small business boom, there is also a huge demand for financial management. Our focus is on QuickBooks Bookkeeping and how it is the best way to earn money in 2021. In the following chapter, we will see how much a bookkeeper earns in the US. What services you can provide as a QuickBooks Bookkeeper, and which cities are the best for practicing QuickBooks bookkeeping.

1.17. 4.1. Salary of Part-Time QuickBooks Bookkeepers

We hear that QuickBooks is a good way to earn money. It is a good side hustle. Be a part-time QuickBooks bookkeeper. No one tells us how much you can make and how much time should be spent to earn a certain amount.

Here we will give you a clear picture of the earnings. A breakdown by weekly, monthly, and yearly earnings.

According to the latest surveys up to 2021, in the United States of America, a QuickBooks bookkeeper's average salary is $50,618 a year. This comes to be around $4,220 per month, around $1000 a week, and about $24 an hour. This sounds very decent for a part-time job. Especially in recent times when we are surrounded by uncertainty, QuickBooks Bookkeeping is a good side hustle.

The figure of $50,618 is the average; it has been reported that you can earn as high as $95,000, and the earnings can even be as low as $29,000. If you want to look at its percentile wise it will look something like this:

- 90th Percentile earnings $93,500 yearly
- 75th Percentile earnings $ 58,500 yearly
- 25th Percentile earnings $ 36,000 yearly

As the survey is based on all kinds of bookkeepers, from entry-level ones to more professional ones, you see a huge income difference. This also suggests that the more experienced and professional abilities you acquire, the higher you will earn.

The following charts must explain the salaries of part-time QuickBooks bookkeepers in a better way.

- The Yearly Average Income of QuickBooks Bookkeepers

- The Average Monthly Income of QuickBooks Bookkeepers

- The Average Weekly Income of QuickBooks Bookkeepers

- The Hourly Average Income of QuickBooks Bookkeepers

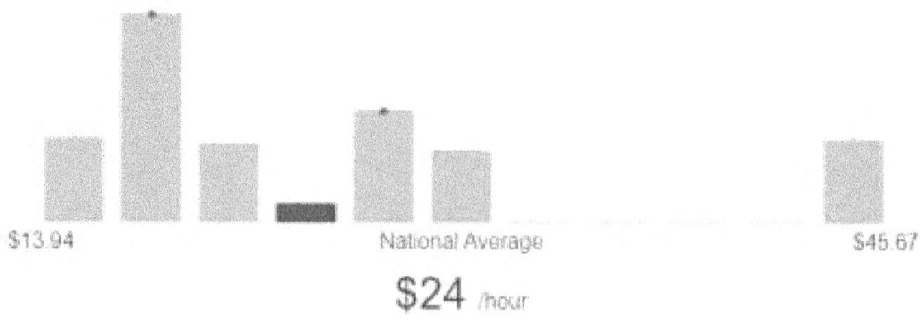

The following table will give you a better understanding of the earning possibilities that come with QuickBooks bookkeeping. These are the results of a recent survey. Thus, they also indicate the present trends as well.

	Annual Salary	Monthly Pay	Weekly Pay	Hourly Wage
Top Earners	$93,500	$7,791	$1,798	$45
75th Percentile	$58,500	$4,875	$1,125	$28
Average	$50,618	$4,218	$973	$24
25th Percentile	$36,000	$3,000	$692	$17

1.18. 4.2. The Top 10 Highest Paying Cities for Bookkeepers in the USA

The survey also indicated that the pay varies from location to location. Here we have compiled the top ten cities in the US where QuickBooks Bookkeepers' salaries are higher than the national average.

The state that offers the highest salaries to the QuickBooks Bookkeepers is, without any doubt, California. Companies in California employ the highest paying QuickBooks bookkeepers. The top salaries are recorded from San Francisco, CA. San Francisco's salaries are around $13,636 higher than the national average. That counts for a whopping 26.9% higher average salary than the average. The second highest is Fremont, CA. The third position is held by San Jose, CA, with a $9,337 higher average salary than the national average of $50,618. Following close behind in Oakland, CA, with an $8,668 higher average. After this is Tanana, AK, with an average yearly salary of $ 59,078, number six is Wasilla, AK, with a higher average of $8459 than the national average. Hayward, CA, has an average income of $58,044 for QuickBooks Bookkeepers. At number eight is Sunnyvale, CA, with an average income higher by $7,268 than the national average. The average salary for this part-time job in Jackson, WY, is $57,870. The last of the tip than in Norwalk, CT.

The table will give you a better understanding of the top ten cities for QuickBooks Bookkeeping.

City	Annual Salary	Monthly Pay	Weekly Pay	Hourly Wage
San Francisco, CA	$64,254	$5,355	$1,236	$30.89
Fremont, CA	$61,596	$5,133	$1,185	$29.61
San Jose, CA	$59,956	$4,996	$1,153	$28.82
Oakland, CA	$59,288	$4,940	$1,140	$28.50
Tanaina, AK	$59,078	$4,923	$1,136	$28.40
Wasilla, AK	$59,077	$4,923	$1,136	$28.40
Hayward, CA	$58,044	$4,837	$1,116	$27.91
Sunnyvale, CA	$57,886	$4,824	$1,113	$27.83
Jackson, WY	$57,870	$4,823	$1,113	$27.82
Norwalk, CT	$57,752	$4,813	$1,111	$27.77

Having mentioned all these cities does not mean that the prospects of getting jobs are higher in these places. This is just an overview of the average income you can earn in these states. Other factors should also be considered when you decide to work in a specific location. For example, you see many six cities from the state of California. You might be tempted to search for work there. But according to research, the job market for QuickBooks Bookkeepers is not active in California. The companies might be paying higher, but the job opportunities are less. It is always smarter to work in a place where the prospects of being employed are better. However, you might be earning more if you locate in one of these locations. It all depends upon the service you provide and the requirements of the employer. It would help if you did your survey before deciding to change your location.

Another important consideration when thinking about making a location change as a QuickBooks bookkeeper is the cost of living. San Francisco may be paying the highest, but the basic cost of living is high. You might be earning more but even spending more on necessities like housing, insurance, and food. This might not prove to be a smart move. For a QuickBooks bookkeeper, an important factor in choosing a location might be the salary and a place with a lower cost of living.

1.19. 4.3. Best Paying QuickBooks Bookkeeping Jobs in the USA

This is true for any field of practice that your job prospects and earnings increase if you specialize in a specific field. This part will discuss the five types of specialized QuickBooks Bookkeepers who earn higher than the typical part-time QuickBooks bookkeepers. All the jobs discuss earn around $7,683 to $14,935 more than the national average. This makes the values about 14.5% to 29.5% more than a regular QuickBooks bookkeeper's salary. So, it is highly recommended that you try to specialize in a certain domain to improve your higher earnings chances. The five jobs we will be discussing are:

1. CPA Firm Bookkeeper
2. QuickBooks Remote Bookkeeper
3. Telecommute Bookkeeper
4. At home Bookkeeper
5. QuickBooks Consultant

4.3.1. CPA Firm Bookkeeper

The Bookkeeper associated with a CPA firm earns around $65,553 annually. This translates to a $5,463 paycheck each month, roughly $1,261 a week. In this case, you will be charging approximately $31.52 an hour. If you consider it seriously, this is quite a decent earning.

4.3.2. QuickBooks Remote Bookkeeper

This job fetches you a whopping $64,952 annual earning. This is more than $14,300 than the national average. You will be earning $5,413 per month, which is decent.

4.3.3. Telecommute Bookkeeper

According to the survey, the Telecommute Bookkeeper earns $60 795 per year. This is $10,000 higher than the national average. This brings you a decent paycheck of $5,000 per month and weekly earnings of $1,000 plus. Working as a telecommute bookkeeper, you will be charging approximately $30 by the hour.

4.3.4. At Home Bookkeeper

The best thing about this type of bookkeeping is that you can practice it from the comfort of your house, and you will be earning good money. You will be making savings on the commute time, fuel expenses, and outside food expenses, if you practice work from home. Continuing from home, you will still be earning $8,000 more than the national average. You will be earning around $5,000 per month from the comfort of your home.

4.3.5. QuickBooks Consultant

As a QuickBooks consultant, you can earn $57,986 per year. The good part about this is that you can work part-time and take home a paycheck of around $5,000 each month.

This table will give you a better understanding of the benefits of specializing and the financial prospects related to it.

Job Title	Annual Salary	Monthly Pay	Weekly Pay	Hourly Wage
CPA Firm Bookkeeper	$65,553	$5,463	$1,261	$31.52
Quickbooks Remote	$64,952	$5,413	$1,249	$31.23
Telecommute Bookkeeper	$60,795	$5,066	$1,169	$29.23
Work From Home Bookkeeper	$58,536	$4,878	$1,126	$28.14
Quickbooks Consultant	$57,986	$4,832	$1,115	$27.88

Chapter 5. Becoming a QuickBooks Bookkeeper

Now that you have a thorough understanding of bookkeeping and QuickBooks, it must be clear that in present times the knowledge of QuickBooks is essential if you want to work in the US small business community. Sometimes learning the software is not enough. To get the job, you require to show some qualifications and expertise as well. Unfortunately, we are still living in the workplace where showing your qualifications and certificates is essential to acquire a job. But when we talk about QuickBooks, there is no harm in doing a certification. Doing a certification will open many opportunities for you. No one wants to hire an unqualified person. With this Certification, you will be considered qualified for the job. The Certification might teach you the software's basics, but the actual learning is always done practically. Nevertheless, gaining this Certification is beneficial even if it gives you a head start.

Sometimes you have this clear picture in your mind regarding what you want to do but you have no access to proper guidance. Many people want to work as bookkeepers and want to learn further to upgrade their skill set but there is no one to guide them. The information around us is so much that sometimes we are overwhelmed by the excess of information rather than its lack. Sometimes all we need is a plain simple instruction in the right direction. This chapter does just that. It will push you one step further in the right direction.

In this chapter, we will discuss how you can gain this Certification, how much it cost, how long it takes to become certified, the difficulty level of this Certification, the types of certifications available for QuickBooks; all will be discussed in this chapter. In this chapter, we will discuss:

- The type of investment required for Certification.
- Different courses available
- Information about QuickBooks Certification.
- The course fees.
- The duration of the course

1.20. 5.1. The Type of Investment Required for Certification

Getting a certification is a big investment. Not only are you investing your money, but you also invest your time and money in such courses as well. In present times, the world is ever-changing and keeping up with the fast-moving times has become mandatory. Otherwise, you will be left behind. Similarly, if you are a bookkeeper, you must upgrade your skillset. You might be employed right now, but what if the employer changes technology and you are no more required to work for him/her, and they hire a person with better qualifications. For such times it is important to be well prepared and keep up with times. Your aim should be to become an asset to the company rather than a liability.

1.21. 5.2. The Different Courses Offered

There are three types of courses offered for QuickBooks Certification. Two of them are for the QuickBooks Desktop, and one is for QuickBooks online. Nowadays, most people prefer a cloud-based financial management system, so it would be wise to take the Certification for the online version. The different types of certifications offered are:

- QuickBooks Online Edition: Basic
- QuickBooks Desktop Edition: Basic
- QuickBooks Desktop Edition: Advanced

1.22. 5.3. Information About QuickBooks Certification

If you are working as an employee, getting a QuickBooks certificate will reassure your employer of your abilities with the software and convince them that you are an asset to their company. Certification will enhance your credibility. This will equip you with the expertise to deal with any situation that involves QuickBooks. You will be in a better position as a QuickBooks certified employee to tackle tricky situations involving QuickBooks.

When you pass the exam, you will gain the following skills, and your certificate will be proof of your abilities:

- Easily use the main measures of QuickBooks and manage business accounts on the software.

- You can manage all the accounting functions like Payroll, transactions, invoices, and sales smoothly with QuickBooks software.
- Can solve and manage complex scenarios that come up while using QuickBooks.

One thing you should keep in mind, the certifications are not cheap, they cost high prices. But you should consider investing in this Certification as a step towards your better career. You will get profits from this investment very soon.

1.23. 5.4. Why Should You Invest

It is a known fact that QuickBooks Certifications do not come cheap. If you are an employer, you might feel that this is a lot of investment, and the courses are time-consuming. If you have many employees, the cost might be an issue for sure. If you are a freelance bookkeeper, the fee might be a big investment. But consider this a useful investment. This is one of the investments you should make. Some business owners consider it an initial investment, and the profits and dividends are gained when the work is done more efficiently and faster.

A lot of groups are offering QuickBooks certification courses. If you are an employer, you can look for bundle package discounts and monthly packages. If you are a freelance service provider, you should look for packages that offer monthly installments as one-time payments are sometimes difficult to pay at once.

You should always look for online courses. Nowadays, many online courses are available, and you can take them from the comfort of your home or office. This can save you the commute expenses and the time which is wasted with the commute. Always look for certifications with live tutoring. These sessions are more interactive, there are live questions and answers sessions, and you learn more this way.

You should be convinced not to take up a QuickBooks certification. If you are still not convinced, maybe this is not for you. But if you want to further your career in bookkeeping, this Certification is essential.

1.24. 5.5. The Certification Fee

Most bookkeepers follow the method that they do their training from a tutor and then take the certification exam. Two groups conduct the Certification:

- Intuit, through their ProAdvisor Program
- NBA (National Bookkeepers Association)

Intuit is the maker of QuickBooks, and they conduct the test for free. However, they cover their cost by making you purchase the mandatory membership, which is hundreds of dollars. You will have to become a member to get access to the test.

NBA conducts the other Certification. This is a much affordable option. If you decide to take the test through them, the fee is $150 for the ones who are taking the test for the first time. This fee includes a practice test and the actual test. At successful completion, you get a certificate. The certification must be updated every year. The fee for each subsequent year is around $75.

1.25. 5.6. The Length of Courses

There is no specific length for courses. The courses and workshops are carried out by professionals who specialize in QuickBooks software. The Certification is only a 2-to-4-hour program. If you are already familiar with the software, you might just book your test and pass. But for someone, the learning might take from weeks to months. All this depends upon few factors:

- Do you have basic knowledge about the software?

In this case, if you have basic knowledge and take the test straight away, the chances are that you might not be able to gain Certification. It would be best if you had more than basic knowledge to pass the Certification. You should not take these exams lightly. Since these exams are expensive, you should prepare your best before taking the exam to get greater chances of passing.

- The Certification you might wish to do.

So, there are different certifications offered. In the Desktop version certifications, there is a basic certificate and an advanced certificate. As the name indicates, the advanced certification will be harder and thus require more expertise.

- When you decide to take the test

You must be responsible when you decide the date to take the test. Do not take the test before you are fully prepared. If you decide the test date before proper preparation, the chances are that you might not be able to pass.

Mostly, the tests can be completed in one sitting. The level of the exams is according to the Certification you wish to do. It is recommended to get the basic Certification before you try to obtain an advanced certification.

Chapter 6. Hacks and Tricks for QuickBooks

With every software, you should know about the tricks and tips to make your work more efficient and streamlined. The same is the case with QuickBooks. You can use the experience of others to better your work. You must have heard the term; time is money, and these tips and tricks save your time. And by saving time, they save your money. In present times we are blessed with technology, and we should try to benefit from t as much as possible. The lives we lead in present times are quite stressful, and the work-life balance is frankly off-balance. In such a situation, it is wise to take as much help as possible. That help can be from technology, or you can even benefit from others' experiences and mistakes. Here we will discuss some hacks and tricks the professionals from the field have agreed upon and shared with everyone to benefit from. Here is a list of a few tricks and hacks to make your work quicker and easier.

The trend of 2021 is focused more on cloud-based QuickBooks software. In this chapter, we will discuss the tips and tricks we can apply in QuickBooks Online to gain better results. We have compiled a list of six hacks that you might find helpful:

- Cash receipts should be created.
- Use attachments.
- Use keyboard shortcuts.
- Automate the emails.
- Use QuickBooks Online to track the time.

- Always use the bank rules

1.26. 6.1. Cash Receipts Should be Created.

It is always a good idea to organize your working space. The same is the case with finances. If you have your cash receipts created and recorded, you will easily overview all money received at any time. With QuickBooks Online, you can enter the details in the sales center and review the records anytime you want. This is a feature of QuickBooks online, which is easy to use and convenient for financial tracking.

- Usage

How you will create cash receipts is simple, go to the sales transactions and create a file med cash receipts. Next, go to the filter list and go to 'Money Received' and enter the date appropriately.

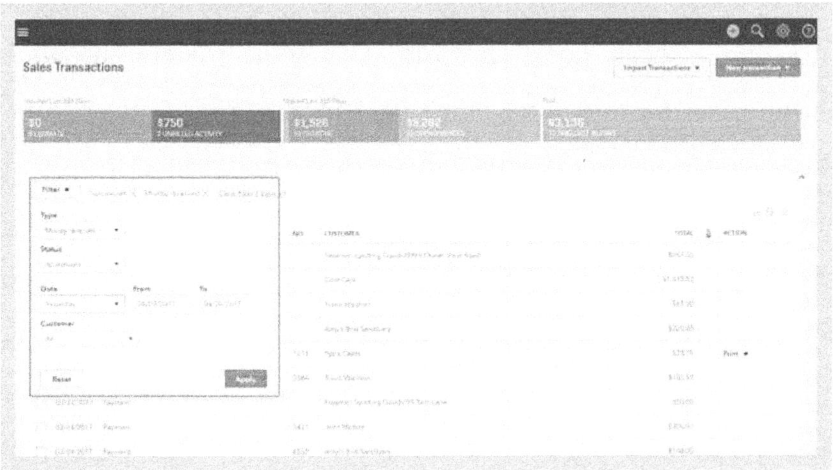

(Cash Receipt Usage)

1.27. 6.2. Use Attachments

This is a hack that is overlooked a lot of the time, and most people ignore using it. The hack is to attach all related forms and documents to the vendor accounts to be managed at once. For example, you can attach a W-9 to the vendor's account.

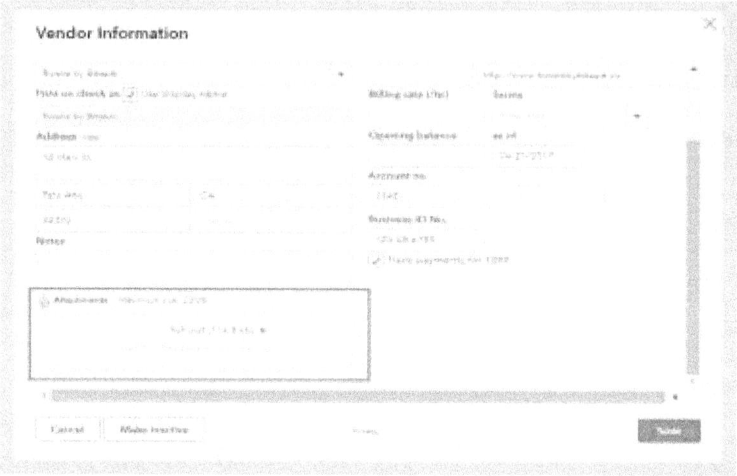

(Using Attachments)

So, when you use attachments, you can also attach the bank accounts' files and the credit card details and statements. When all the documents are attached and compiled in one place, they will be easy to review. Another pro tip will be to use naming conventions. This will make the work more streamlined and easier to track. According to experts, not using attachments wastes time you could be spending on other activities. There is no need to work so hard if you have applications in your software that make your work easier and smoother to operate. If you are using a mobile version of QuickBooks online, you can even take a screenshot of any receipt and attach it to the folder. In the same way, you can even attach the invoices and enter the yearly or monthly estimates. If you have the add-on of QuickBooks Payments, you can even receive payments.

1.28. 6.3. Use Keyboard Shortcuts

This is also a huge time saver. When you are working on multiple things, clicking from one program to another makes everything confusing. The same is the case with QuickBooks. When you are managing multiple entities, you need to work fast, and shortcuts are a lifesaver. Following is a summary of all the important shortcuts found within QuickBooks.

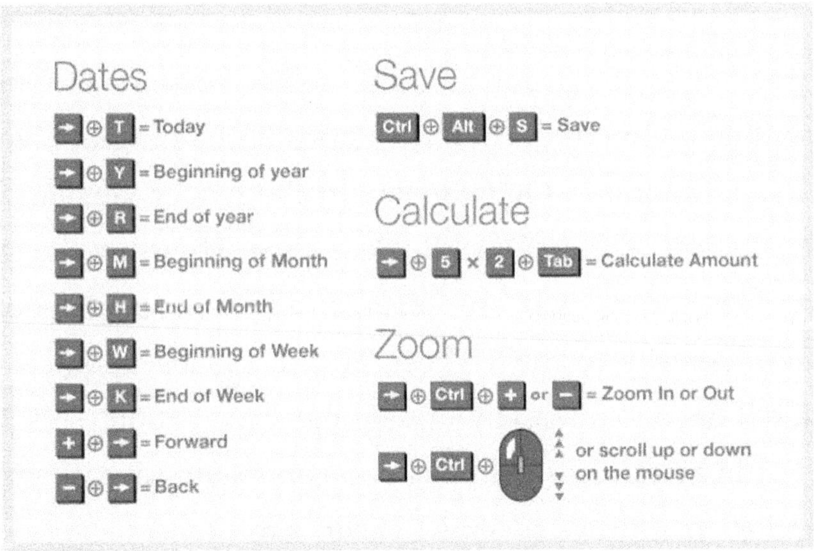

(QuickBooks shortcuts)

1.29. 6.4. Automate the emails.

For all the regular payments and receiving, automation is the way to go. You should automate your emails for sales, financial statements, and invoices. You must be thinking about how to go about this? It is easy; you will first set different reports scheduled to email on a specific date. For example, you can set a schedule that emails you your financial statement monthly. You can even get an email for the collection report, and the sales report every week. This will help you keep track of the open invoices.

Apart from this, you can schedule the payments that have to be sent out weekly or monthly. You can arrange for the recurring invoices to be sent automatically by email. Again, if you use the app QuickBooks payments, the received payments can be automatically recorded automatically.

1.30. 6.5. Use the QuickBooks Online to Track Time

If time tracking is tough for you, the newer versions of QuickBooks Online will help you. In the older versions of the program, you had to import the T reports to QuickBooks. In the newer versions, you can create the T sheets within QuickBooks online. These are the integrated T sheets. This means that any change, addition, or deletion would apply automatically to the T sheet, and it will be updated by itself. You will not have to manually update the information. This process is carried out in a seamless manner. You can create several employee T sheets and even approve several T sheets simultaneously.

1.31. 6.6. Always use the Bank Rules

This is a simple and logical hack. The bank rules are already made, and time tested. If you implement them and set your regular payments to the utilities, vendors, suppliers, etc., on bank rules, the task will become easier. This can save a lot of time for you as well. At the end of the month, all you will need to do is an overview of all the payments carried out in a smooth and streamlined fashion.

These hacks and tips may seem simple but implementing them can save you hours and hours' worth of labor. There will be far fewer things on your mind. It is a one-time setup, and it will be automated from then on. You will easily manage the payments, receiving, employee timesheets, Payroll, and everything else with ease, and you will become less stressed.

Chapter 7. QuickBooks Usage in Small Businesses

Many small businesses use QuickBooks to manage their finances. The software takes care of their bill payments, monitors their cash flow, and manages invoices. QuickBooks is a good software to generated automated monthly financial reports as well as yearly financial reports. Some business owners manage their accounts themselves and are pro users of the software, but most business owners employ professionals to manage their accounts. QuickBooks certified bookkeepers are employed by small to mid-size business owners to manage their accounts.

Small business owners use QuickBooks for several functions and use. Following are the functions for which the small business owners use QuickBooks:

- Make and track invoices.
- Monitor expenses and other bills.
- Generate business and financial statements.
- Manage payroll.
- Do the inventory.
- Simplify taxes.
- Online payments.
- Record Receipts.

- Manage mileage.

1.32. 7.1. Make and Track Invoices

The software has the option to create invoices, and you can easily print them or directly send them to your customers. Each invoice generated by the software will be automatically recorded in the system. In this way, you can track all the amount that has already been paid, and the receivables will also be displayed.

1.33. 7.2. Monitor Expenses and Other Bills

You have an option to link the QuickBooks software to your accounts and credit cards. This will enable the program to record all payments and bills automatically and keep a record. It will be available for your view whenever you require.

You can enter other bills you receive in the system and take care of the payables. This will help you keep track of your expenses and payables. The software will make sure you do not miss your payments. If you attach the QuickBooks payment app, the payments can even be managed automatically.

1.34. 7.3. Generate Business Financial Statements

The software can generate financial statements that will give you an overview of your business performance. The kind of statements you can generate with the QuickBooks software are:

- Cashflow Statement
- Profit and Loss Statement

- Balance Sheets

1.35. 7.4. Manage Payroll

The software can manage the Payroll and working hours of each employee automatically. You must create a separate account for each employee, enter each employee's information, and schedule the salary, deductions, schedules, and hours. All can be managed automatically by the software. If you use the software, you can easily manage:

- Payment to the employees can be made by checks or cash.
- The taxes can be deducted automatically, and the tax-exempt employee payments are also managed.
- The software fills tax forms automatically
- The payroll taxes can be managed automatically.

1.36. 7.5. Do the Inventory.

The software manages the inventory. It records the quantities and keeps track of the total cost of inventory. The software will indicate when the inventory is getting low, and there is a need to replenish. This all is not done automatically, you will have to enter the amounts manually, but they will be managed and calculated automatically.

1.37. 7.6. Simplify Taxes

Taxes is one of the most difficult parts of the business. Most people are fearful of taxes, and in the end, their taxes are piled up. QuickBooks takes care of your taxes. The Tax becomes difficult because your financial statements are not in order. QuickBooks makes the financial statements simplified, and you can easily print them out and let a tax preparer assess the statements and use the required information.

1.38. 7.7. Online Payments

The QuickBooks Payments app enables you to accept payments directly from your customers. This app is integrated into the software, so all the payments are recorded in the system automatically.

1.39. 7.8. Record Receipts

The QuickBooks app makes it possible for the business owner to upload all the payment and expense receipts to the software, and they can be easily scanned and recorded in the system.

1.40. 7.9. Manage Mileage

If you use your vehicle for business purposes, a tax deduction is applied. But to receive the tax deduction, you will have to prove your traveling. You get a deduction of 57.5 cents per mile. To record the miles, you can link QuickBooks Online to your vehicle's GPS, and it will easily record your miles, date, and time

Conclusion

If you have read the whole book, many of your doubts must have been cleared regarding bookkeeping and QuickBooks. This is an amazing opportunity for you to avail yourself if you want to take up bookkeeping as a profession. It is always a better idea to keep up with the current trends and technology because it ensures better job and working opportunities. Therefore, we have mentioned QuickBooks. Being a QuickBooks certified bookkeeper gives you an edge in business. This is because most small to mid-size businesses have installed the QuickBooks software for their financial management. There are different versions of QuickBooks available:

- QuickBooks Self-Employed
- QuickBooks Online
- QuickBooks Desktop
- QuickBooks Apps

QuickBooks is user-friendly and is compatible with other programs like MS Word and MS excel. Different versions are available that are compatible with iOS, android, windows, and Mac operating systems.

It will be a good idea to specialize in cloud-based QuickBooks software because, as of 2014, more and more business owners are interested in keeping their records on the cloud-based package offered by QuickBooks. If you are planning to get your Certification any time soon, the cloud-based product should be your focus. There is a basic course offered in QuickBooks Online; you should consider that.

Another consideration when thinking about QuickBooks bookkeeping seriously is what type of Bookkeeper you are going to be. According to a survey, these five types of part-time QuickBooks bookkeepers are making the highest number of average incomes:

- CPA Firm Bookkeeper
- QuickBooks Remote Bookkeeper
- Telecommute Bookkeeper
- At home Bookkeeper
- QuickBooks Consultant

The next most important point to think about is your location. At different locations in America, bookkeepers make different yearly incomes. The QuickBooks bookkeepers make the highest yearly earnings in San Francisco, California. But before quickly packing your bags towards the sunny state, keep in mind the expenses as well. Before shifting your location, always consider the basic expenses and how you will be managing them. It may be possible that you are earning less in one city, but the cost of living is cheaper, and in another city, you might be making more money, but the expenses are equally higher. In the latter case, you end up losing more money. So, always take a well-thought-out and informed decision.

In all, if you are someone good with numbers and have a consistent work ethic, you can very manage to be a QuickBooks bookkeeper.

You can even work as a freelance service provider. Providing services is also generally a risk-free approach. The only investment you make is the training you do and the courses you take. After that, all is gain. In this way, you can set your schedule and take up as much work as you can manage. In present times where the future has become unpredictable, freelancing is the way to go.

Lightning Source UK Ltd.
Milton Keynes UK
UKHW052004150321
380411UK00006B/997

9 781802 242898